Maggiedocious Wordette's

Soul Sonnets

Spoken Word Book

by John Gary Dewberry
Co-Author K. Sylvia

Copyright © 2025

by John Gary Dewberry and Co-Author K. Sylvia. All rights reserved.

No part of this publication may be reproduced, distributed, or transmitted in any form or by any means, including photocopying, recording, or other electronic or mechanical methods, without the prior written permission of the author or publisher, except in the case of brief quotations embodied in critical reviews and certain other non-commercial uses permitted by copyright law. For bulk purchases, please contact John Gary Dewberry at mycybermap@gmail.com

Pa-Pro-Vi Publishing www.paprovipublishing.com

Printed in the USA

ISBN# 978-1-959667-60-5

CONTENTS

FOREWORD IV
ACKNOWLEDGEMENTS VI
INTRODUCTION X

SOUL SONNET #1
The Christmas Connoisseur 2

SOUL SONNET #2
42g – XY & Me 27

SOUL SONNET #3
Savante Muse 53

SOUL SONNET #4
Barack, Baroque 76

SOUL SONNET #5
My First Christmas Away From Home 101
EPILOGUE 122
AFTERWORD 1244
BIOGRAPHY 126

Foreword

I have watched a King grow, love passionately, fall, get up, and move forward for many years. He is a distinctive innovator, able to see beyond, imagine what seems impossible, and with determination, can bring a thought to reality.

My husband has always been a forward thinker. This is a gift from God. He will tell you that all the things accomplished in his life he would not have been able to do without his Faith in the Lord. John will tell you that he takes credit for nothing; he surrenders daily to God, who governs his life. He knows that he can do all things through Jesus Christ who strengthens him. (Philippians 4:13 NKJV)

John has a love for the English language. He is witty and quick with his tongue in a good way (LOL). He can bring forth words from the depth of his soul and invite the reader into his imagination, placing the words on the canvas and inviting the reader to leap inside the time capsule of the story and enjoy the excitement of what comes next. Soul Sonnets will take you on a captivating journey through poetry. This is truly poetry in motion as the words dance off the page as you read. Some might say that it will move you to worship, praise, sing, and pray.

As the author's wife, I've seen the intricate details and heard the thought processes and plans for this book. The most prominent point I have listened to is John's passion and caring for his readers. Maggiedocious Wordette is a distinctive innovation. Hop on this soulful ride of rhythmic laughs, cries, joy, love, peace, and chicken grease. The beginning, middle, and end will captivate your very soul.

My soulmate! Best friend of 50 years and married for 9 years. We love the Lord, walk in sync, and believe what Jesus said in Mark 9:23 (NKJV): Jesus said to him, "If you can believe, all things are possible to him who believes." Amen.

Acknowledgements

Thank God for the gift of Jesus Christ. Thank you to my wife, Karen Sylvia (Ware) Dewberry for your support, inspiration and poetic justice. Thank you to my parents, who Rest in Eternal Peace with the Lord. My mother Irene and Father John Gary Dewberry Sr., who provided me with those wonderful encyclopedias in the 1970's while growing up, they challenge words and facts, saying look it up! Rest In Peace, Black Historian/Teacher Ruth Ethel Dennis, (my wife's grandmother) thank you for your book, *The Black People in America* and your records that teach Black History.

Thank you to your daughter (my mother-in-law, Rest In Peace) Renee Francine Dennis (Ware), a renowned teacher in Springfield, Massachusetts, respected in Decatur Georgia, who I know in my heart gets a real big kick out of me becoming an Ordain Pastor 2023 and incorporating her daughter's (my wife) poetry into a book. Thank you, Rodman K. Ware, (Rest in Peace, father-in-law) for blessing my marriage to your daughter and blessing me as a man and a Minister of God. Thank you, Joyce H. (Harvey) Ware (Stepmother), for showing me your book *Common-Law wife* and encouraging me to become an author and Minister of God, (Rest in Eternal Peace). Thank you everyone who bought my first book Hang All The Mistletoe, Meet The Black Ebenezer, especially those who asked for an autographed copy.

Maggiedocious Wordette's Soul Sonnets

Thank you, Aunt D (my wife's Godmother), Thank you, Ms. Rachel Alexander for reading the book more than once and telling me about it. Thank you, Cheryl (Ninky 7) Cook, for reading the whole book and honestly assessing it as *good*. Thank you Pearlie Marie (Maria) Egerton-Pinkett for ordering my book from Walmart. Thank you, Anita Ware Johnson (Sister-In-Law), for ordering my book online, thank you, Darryl Benson (Dew wrote a book, I gotta get it). Thank you, Regina Tillman for your Press advice.

Thank you, Lawrence "Larry" Allen, (Great book Dew). Thank you, Mark C. Holmes, Tony Holmes and the Holmes Family, Thank you Larry Hallums and your beautiful daughter Amanda Hallums-Burrell. Thank you, Grace Dyson, for buying my book, Thank you to my 1978 High School of Commerce classmates, and Scott Walker. Thank you to my Niece Nakia Dewberry M. ED. for writing the Foreword for my first book, Hang All the Mistletoe, Meet the Black Ebenezer Scrooge.

Thank you to my Brother Stanley Dewberry for buying two books, thank you Lacresha Carter (Myles and Baliegh) for buying four books. Thank you to Gwen Richardson of the National Black Book Festival, Fallbrook Church Houston, Tx. Thank you, New Back Wallstreet Atlanta, Ga. and Privi at Stonecrest Mall, Stonecrest Ga. Thank you, LaQuita Parks, Pa-Pro-Vi Publishing.

Thank you, Amy Cancryn Firebrand Publishing, thank you Renita Bryant, Mynd Matters Publishing. My music background for the year+ that it took to write Soul Sonnets I and II was the year 2000 Jazz album from Detroit's own violinist Regina Carter, titled Motor City Moments.

Thank you, Andrew Cade, ("not the size of the ship that make it rock") Nathaniel "Nat" Sanders (John, you had me hooked with your mention of a Radio Station) for kind words of encouragement, Wellington Allen, Craig Chapman, Neville Waters and the late great Deighton Alleyn (Rest In Eternal Peace) for College radio DJ training, music mastery and Personality. I thank God for each of you mentoring and molding my business and personal life.

Thank you, Terry "TE" Eddy, you are Iron that sharpens, my brother, Peace to you. Thank you Deacon Arenzo O. Washington my great friend and brother. Brother Minister, Thank you to you and your wife Cynthia for your support and promotion. Thank you, Minister Duane Nelson and your wife Glenda, for your promotion and support. Thank you, Minister Kevin A. Green (CEO of Seeds of a Father) Founder of Get Ya Health Up Initiative for pre-ordering my first book.

Thank you, Gigi Griffin, Beulah Singleton (my sister) Leronia Clay (Counselor) Mother Fae Carr James, the Faith of a Mustard Seed Prayer Line, and Mother Carolyn Saffo.

I give Thanks for Riverside Baptist Church, Pastor and Co-Pastor Lloyd and Jennifer Key, and Salt and Light

Truth Center, Bishop Deitric Avery, both in Decatur, Ga.

Thank you, Elder Kevin Vaughan, of Kingdom Works International Ministries, Conyers, Ga. for God's Wisdom, leadership and advice, thank you Men's Let's Talk Network.

Thank you Dr. Deborah Harrell-Isom and husband Minister Vernon Isom for your leadership in my 2023 Ordination from AARON'S BEARD International School of Ministry and Begin Again Ministries Inc. Peachtree City, Ga.

INTRODUCTION

John Gary Dewberry presents Maggiedocious Wordette's Soul Sonnet's Holidays

Welcome to Maggiedocious Wordette's Soul Sonnet Holiday's, a Black Girl Magic Poetry Slam connecting rhythm to rhyme, woman to woman, with men cheering on the sidelines. Write-on. She is The Ghost of Christmas Past, a key to the future, a gift that keeps on giving, she's moving, she's grooving, wrapping until the music book stops now, Yeah!

Maggiedocious Wordette is every Black woman, a super soul sister who helps the intended recapture the spiritual glow of life, early Christmas morning in the dark of night.

Maggiedocious Wordette is an open book, if you look, she jumped out of the pages of the Christmas book *"Hang All The Mistletoe" Meet The Black Ebenezer Scrooge,* shining bright like the North Star. She is the Queen of yesterday's dreams, so pretty her skin glows and Afro flows, shaped like Africa her body goes, when she speaks it's always in prose.

Maggiedocious speaking in prose, which means I rhyme and connect thoughts all the time, not living in the past revealing defeats but offering insight to ensure bad decisions won't repeat.

Hear is a spoken word written by Maggiedocious Wordette titled The Butterfly Effect, to see the Cause and Effect in chapter 5. Wordette makes waves

Maggiedocious Wordette's Soul Sonnets

beginning to end, never-ending, giving to the notion that emotions of Christmases past lay in each day, until Christmas Present fades away.

A Sonnet is a poem of 14 lines, using various forms of rhymes in a rhythmic scheme to express an idea or a theme. Soul Sonnet poetry uses various forms of rhymes in a rhythmic scheme to expound on an idea or a theme, not through 14 lines do I exact thought, 14 pages, giving you the best I got.

The Soul Sonnet force explores thought space like satellites escape the bonds of gravity, blast of from the Nativity, we come in peace like America's Space Force, no longer a joke or vanity. Space Jam is a cartoon, but looney is the tune, if the plan is a Massah plantation as a sky platoon.

Make room on your bookshelf, take me home, give Soul Sonnets a place to roam, free your Mind and the love will follow.

Maggiedocious Wordette, a soulful Love Guru to you, taken out of nowhere to be, now here.

The Christmas Connoisseur

Hang All the Mistletoe I'm going to get to know you better, you shall get to know me better too. We toast the planet host who does the most, sealed by a holy kiss, different than a mistletoe kiss, or a wish to kiss your significant other, with a French kiss.

Speaking in tongue doesn't have to be a mystery, the attraction is mutual, as is mutual edification of holy tongues speaking life one to one. Each one pledging to reach another one, and how else can you hear the Word, but by the preaching of the Word.

Madame or Mademoiselle, to properly hail a French female, Monsieur be you male, married or single, dispersed over the entire world, Africa does mingle, co-mingle but who's zooming who.

Entanglement is the truth hidden in plain sight, the French province of Africa was not a one-night stand, they fell in love forever with Morrocco, Mauritius and twenty-nine Countries including Cote d' Ivoire, sure by colonization more speak Francois by the seashore.

Ah toast to Djibouti! A country that gained its independence in 1977 but speaks French that began to entrench by Colony in 1626. France got in on the dirty dance, joining the mad scramble of the worlds' egg heads, to colonize Africa in 1830.

Maggiedocious Wordette

A bit of Sarah Dash, Patti LaBelle, Nona Hendrix, mocha chocolata ya, ya, sings of the frenzy with proper sheet music, in a 1974 hit record by Labelle, titled Lady Marmalade.

Marmalade is a fruit preserve made from the juice and peel of citrus fruits boiled with sugar and water, it's not jam but it shakes like jelly. Orange Marmalade is not made for French toast that does the most to pick you up, matched with hot butter and maple syrup.

French toast goes well with champagne and orange juice, called Mimosa, a perfect dialect for a new day to begin, like diamonds are a girl's best friend.

My dearest love - Ma Cherie d'amour, - French translation.

Africa is the place to find every Gem, but you can't trust a big promise and a smile, digging a hole into the Mother Land is spiritually forbidden and a lie, when hidden behind a negligee of sex, lies and videotape, showing the naked truth. Being a dominatrix is no alibi.

The champagne campaign of tiny bubbles in the wine is a French thing found in 1531, but no one had any fun until 1844 when Adolphe Jacquesson perfected a wire cage to keep the cork in place.

Poppin bottles into space didn't hurt anyone anymore, which is a good thing since corks popping off premature had a dangerous way of making champagne drinking a dodgeball sport.

The champagne game is on lock in Champagne France, located in the Northeast region of the Country, known as the wine region. Wine can only be legally called champagne if it is bottled within 100 miles of the Champagne region.

Europeans have influenced the world in many things, accentuating the feminine body with body shaping wear. Body shaping clothing was introduced during the 1550's by the wife of French King Henry II, Catherine de Medici, who wanted size 13 waists on all woman at Royal events, women were tied up with rod enforced panels of cloth, to achieve this shape.

This idea, brought from Italy, would eventually be called a corset by the French in 1820 and this Elizabethan Era beauty regime was enforced by high society for 400 years, 1550 to 1950 but considered torture by women, without pity. You've come a long way lady, to get where you got too today, relieved during the Victorian age of Queen Victoria 1840 to 1901, Victoria's secret is underwear, to have more fun.

Say it with your chest, gets a bustier, a corset trims the waist, a bustier accentuates the Busts but World War I was the demise of corset ambition, because more metal was needed for ammunition.

Mary Phelps Jacob, a Socialite from New York City changed the Times in 1913, inventing the modern bra, which is short for brasserie, some ladies give it the Bronx cheer.

France is known around the world for art, architecture, fashion, cuisine and literature
*La France est connue dans le monde entier pour son art, son architecture, sa mode, sa cuisine et sa litterature.

Thanks, Vivienne Westwood, for reclaiming my time in the 1950's, not Auntie Maxine Water's political kind but female power, sexual and otherwise, to reconceptualize the corset, bring it into the modern set.

Thank Heaven for little girls, thank Heaven for them all, no matter where, no matter who without them what would little boys do? Thank Heaven, thank Heaven. Thank Heaven for little girls. The ending of a classic song sung by Mourice Chevelier in 1958, for the movie Gigi.

Gigi is a young lady that becomes a beautiful woman right before the eyes of a rich playboy who was just a friend, but now wants her to become his new playgirl. Gigi is no silly rabbit; she will not give in unless she's married to him, ooh la la la, she wins in the end.

Provocative but true, what you won't do for love, a supercalifragilisticexpialidocious woman will make you do for love, what you would not do.

Super-docious woman, extraordinarily good, she can make caviar wishes and champagne dreams come true! Who is that? Maggiedocious Wordette that's who!

Maggiedocious is the imagination of a woman. Yes, she can make dreams come true, show you the heart of Christmas Past, validate the Present, align the Future, even make you laugh.

And it's a man's man's world, but it would be nothing, nothing, not one little thing, without a woman or a girl, sung in 1966 by the Godfather of Soul, timeless Black gold, it never gets old.

And these are a few of my favorite things: I like the color burgundy, and burgundy wine. I like the chocolatier who makes the cocoa bean fine, a Makeup Artist that blends perfectly Rouge, and Brandy is another wine. I like the Eiffel Tower, built in 1887 and finished in 1889.

And you can believe the Past, no stifle when you see it in a tower standing tall in Paris, France, Iron fused in lattice to sharpen your glance at a wonder of the world, built by Gustave Eiffel.

The Grand Cathedral is built to last, begun in year 1163, opened in 1345, taking 182 years to build, still it thrives in the New Millennium. Its name, Notre Dame de Paris, a Roman Catholic Church famous for stained glass windows, dedicated to Virgin Mary, it is a Holy place on Earth.

Maggiedocious Wordette

I'm ready, Helen Reedy, **I am woman hear me roar, in numbers too big to ignore and I know too much to go back and pretend cause I've heard it all before.**

'Our Lady of Paris' - Notre-Dame De Pari

And don't you say maybe the virgin Mother Mary of Northern Africa had a Holy Baby, it was Jesus she did carry. Now see His Happy Bornday, changed the Times from BC to AD.

Maggiedocious Wordette is your Christmas wake up call. WayAAACupp! to the content of the character of the Waymaker, our gift born of a Woman, conceived by the Will of God.

You are not odd if you find that unbelievable. Life can be hard, and we can be our own worst enemy, believing the deceiver, not giving of ourselves to become receivers of a gift from God.

In a Spike Lee School Daze, wait till they get a load of me plowing seeds on a big screen the size of 40 Acres, with a mule that takes the hump out of his back to do the Camel Walk. Stilettos for these toes, Carmex for these juicy lips, this is my Christmas pep talk every year and someone new will find anew, Jesus is real love, The New Testament of God is truth.

Rejoicing in the gift of Eternal Life will bring strife to the deceiver, causing him to rob and steal would-be believers of joy on Christmas Day. Not seeing it as Soul for Real, or Kid and Play but for the love of money, tho a girl likes nice gifts, a woman does also, Cause Diva's get lonely too.

Christmas Past is a task for all who may forget the miracle, then use disappointment as a false Prophet's ointment. The deceiver's unholy appointment to keep us from the truth of present day, take the fun away from an Eternal gift that keeps giving, when yesterday is done.

The Christmas connoisseur, a distinguished curator of all things Christmas, a savant servant of what your needs be, I'm every woman. A connoisseur is an expert on a subject who appreciates details big and small, call us expert helpers, where it's at and what it is!

Maggiedocious Wordette, the Christmas connoisseur of the best time of the year. We don't need another hero, I'm the protector of the pleasure principle that ended BC and made it Ground Zero.

In 1582 a new Gregorian calendar you invent, to count the days we wait for our ship to come in, call it Advent, to see the North Star Shine on the Messiah God sent.

Christmas is the day hopelessness ends, the Times of the world begin again, no more counting backwards to find Him, Jesus is a new beginning.

By Jesus, God and sinner are reconciled –
*Par Jesus, Dieu et pecheur sont reconcilies

Maggiedocious Wordette

Africa is the Motherlode, within its land flows every mineral, it is the cradle of the world from which all things flow.

Take it to the bridge... the land bridge, 14 thousand years before Christ was born, oceans were different then, you could do the walk from the Motherland to other lands, and people found new world beaches of fine sand.

Go to 1619, oh say can you see Africans arriving from across the Sea, the land where God created the Garden of Eden, where they say God is African. Where all things of Africa are African, and there is no Middle East in the name plan.

Let Maggiedocious Wordette find a perfect Christmas gift to give a woman who has everything, a man too, young or old, anyone can relate, who are about to seriously date.

Check out this book titled "The Street" by Ann Petry written in 1946, don't worry about the date it's timeless like the "1619 Project" authored by Nikole Hannah-Jones, done in 2021.

Ann Petry, born in Old Saybrook Ct. October 12th, 1908, living until April 28th, 1997, believes in heaven, she is the first Black woman to sell 1-Million books in America, her subjects, esoterica.

She was inducted into the Connecticut Woman's Hall of Fame in 1994, ain't no shame, women wait years for the same recognition as men, readers know the ladies have talent and ambition.

Ann Petry knows dreaming of a white Christmas, and I'll be home for Christmas, her book is not a Christmas story, it's called the Black Woman's "Soul on Ice" a reference to the classic written by Eldridge Cleaver in 1968, to Civil Rights her writing relates. "The Street" is about the plight of a Black woman and a Black man's fight to love each other setting a tone that 22 years into the future, "Soul on Ice" would expand on.

Nutty Professor 2, Sherman Klump becomes Joe College in the movie and wants a wife that's hot like the sands of the new world islands found in 1492, by Christopher Columbus' hands. Columbus sailed from Spain to discover the West Indies, not America, as it has been claimed, Natives were there with Caribbean queens aplenty.

Bold Black Beautiful Woman - *Belle femme noire audacieuse

Spain and France would claim all the territories they found by shipping lanes; they changed the world game. La Florida in 1513 they did name, explorer Jean Ponce de Leon came from Spain and is credited as the official discoverer, a precursor for European immigrants, the world knows and Black history laments.

Maggiedocious Wordette

Ponce de Leon's chase of the fountain of youth was rumored to be on an island called Bimini, which turned out to be La Florida. But when he went back in 1521 the Natives were restless, Ponce de Leon died in a battle to get ashore, and the conquest of Bimini was no more.

In 1562 Jean Ribault was sent from France to explore La Florida, to begin a new colony, but he could not win. In 1564 Rene Goulaine de Laudonniere tried in vain to walk in enchanted waters of Heaven's fountain of youth, but uncovered no such thing, of that there was no truth.

Florida is Bimini, there's Land O' Lakes, Saint Augustine Park, the Panhandle bend, Tallahassee and Jacksonville on the other end. Maimi heat and the Florida Keys islands are the farthest point South in the United States, the fountain of youth can be found in the breeze of the sunshine state.

Santa Claus and Bimini are rumors based on truth.

Santa is Saint Nicholas, a Bishop of the Church, who lived from March 15th AD 270 to December 6th 343. He was born in Myra Türkiye and worked for people, to live their best lives, secretly giving money and gifts to the needy, during the Winter Solstice.

The Christmas Connoisseur

"We can dance underwater and not get wet" doing the Aqua boogie from "Motor Booty Affair" the 1978 Album by Parliament Funkadelic. George Clinton keeps on bringing the P-Funk, with another underwater trip in the 2019 album "Right Down #1 Bimini Road."

The fountain of youth would be a nice Christmas gift, a fantasy you can receive, Christmas Day is here or on the way, in that the faithful do believe.

Florida is probably the first French speaking State of the U.S.A- *La Floride est probablement le premiere Etat francophone des U.S.A

Colonization of Florida proved to be tricky, Europeans collaborate with Natives, but the relationship gets sticky and not because of hot weather. Goodwill gets cold, the Natives weapons were old, they put up a fight, but the weapons of supremacy were worth their weight in gold.

Florida becomes the twenty-seventh State of the Union of the United States of America, after our heroic victory over the British army in war called Revolutionary. The Revolutionary war was fought from April 19th, 1775, to September 3rd, 1783, **My Country Tis of Thee.**

America was born on July 4th, 1776, that's one thousand seven hundred and seventy-six years after the birth of Christmas. The Christmas Connoisseur will drink to that, a sip of Courvoisier from Cognac, France, a town founded near the year AD 900, this is a historical fact, pour it over ice, let it chill like that.

The Christmas Connoisseur brings forth logistic history, to connect dates, years and facts in a Soul Sonnet, to take away the mystery of the Spirit of Christmas Past.

The first Cognac house was found in 1643, then perfected by Jean Martell on the scene in 1715. This pristine wine can only be called Cognac if it is double distilled white grapes, you will only find in the Charente, Charente-Maritime region of France.

Cognac became famous when bottled and shipped around the world in 1847 by Denis Mounie and Jules Robin, who give a new liquor and meaning to the phrase, bottle popping.

Standing on the shore of hope watching wave after wave land on the beach of emotions, good sad or bad, with memories of all we had, now under the sway of evil hands, wicked demands.

When your ship comes in, it fills you for a lifetime. For the people of God this Day is our lifeline to Heaven. God and sinner reconciled; Christ Thy Savior is born.

I say again, see the prosperity of that long-awaited Christmas Day, and see the Good News Ship called Redemption, once far off, docking in the Bay.

Water is life - *L'eau est la vie

The Christmas Connoisseur

Ship Ahoy!

It's not the size of the ship that makes it rock, it tis the rolling motion of the mighty ocean.

Take a trip on this Relation Ship, like a Minnie Riperton sound wave "Inside My Love" done in 1975, soul surreal it's a fantasy that makes you feel alive, no jive, Adventures in Paradise.

Who's that lady? *"You can look yeah, but don't touch"* The Isley Brothers in 1973 did sing.

Maggiedocious will make you jump ship man, a woman, full grown and sweet to kiss, man cupid's arrow didn't miss, man big hair, don't care, natural or perm, not a slave to the rhythm, my love you've got to earn, man. Screw your wig on tight, takes care of business day and night, put the winter festival on ice, every night is Ladies Night, man. Sugar and spice and everything nice, man. The Ghost of Christmas Past, a present-day gift of Eternal life, man.

R-E-S-P-E-C-T the queen of Soul Sonnets, Maggiedocious Wordette who makes a cold case, listen to Aretha Franklin sing Amazing Grace, feel the spirit of Christmas take its rightful place.

Christmas can get lost when you don't know the facts. Soul Sonnets rhyme in a timeline, go back and forth, some have questions like how much is the Silver on King Solomon's porch worth?

How much is knowledge worth? Where was Christmas before Christ came to earth?

Maggiedocious Wordette

The Tower of Bable is where God scattered the Tribe, this is not a guess, it's how you interpret spiritual context, Genesis is the beginning of the Bible, of that there is no contest.

Let us go to, God said to the Word of God, who is Jesus, to see what they have built, and seeing God would scatter the 12 families of Jacob around the world, each now having their own tongue, no longer speaking the same language, that's all done.

Footsteps are ordered, set by The Holy Spirit to get back together, only by hearing Jesus' name. Alpha and Omega, the beginning and the end. Focus on Alpha Christmas, The New Testament of God begins, count backwards from 33 BC to zero, see AD 1, count forward until you see AD 33.

My ship has come in, my fortune is made – *Mon navire est arrive, ma fortune est fiat.

Ship Ahoy!

Another ship is landing, this one with tobacco, alcohol and spices. Ships will have to do, since the Oceans have changed the constitution of Continents, and the Worlds constituents, but you cannot discover land that's already been uncovered.

Tempted by the fruit of another, as Indian Princess Pocahontas, found in 1619 Jamestown, Virginia by John Smith, an Englishman who thought he found I dream of Jeanie, pun intended.

The Indians ran out of runway, to say it again, they got bulldozed out of the way, take it to the land bridge that allowed people from the Mother Land to walk to other lands before the oceans reclaim the soil.

The Indians were restless again when found by ships from Spain, each one with a female name Nina, Pinta and Santa Maria, then facts get turned around like hounds do trying to catch a fox and we the people get brainwashed. He who has the gold makes the rules, the victors make the rules, winners of the battles of war can change the score, and all of them do.

Christopher Columbus never made it to the North American mainland, history said he discovered America, but the Christmas Connoisseur gives the Indians of North America a history hug.

It is said if you love someone set them free, if they come back, then their love for you is true Maggiedocious says truth will make you free. To be set free implies that you could be caught again, but whom Christmas makes free is free indeed.

John Lennen and Yoko Ono wrote "So This Is Christmas" in 1971, this song moves everyone.

And so, this is Christmas for weak and for strong, for rich and the poor ones, the world is so wrong. And so happy Christmas, for black and for white, for yellow and red ones let's stop all the fight.

A very Merry Christmas and a happy New Year, let's hope it's a good one without any fear.

The Love Boat, love exciting and new, come aboard.

*Le Love Boat, l'amour passionate et nouveau, embarquez monotint a bord

Ship Ahoy!
There's no fuss about the Pilgrims landing on Plymouth Rock, in Plymouth Massachusetts, better said, they didn't land on Plymouth Rock, Plymouth Rock landed on us.

The captain of the Mayflower was Christopher Jones, not Columbus, who brought 132 souls from England in 1620, that's 148 years after Columbus landed in the Caribbean Islands in 1492.

Women go everywhere that men went, like traveling in twos on Noah's Ark and we are back to Genesis where time starts moving forward, carrying the Lord's Ark. Women are nurturers, giving spiritual information to the people, each a Nation of seeds like stars filling the heavens, and our terrible two-year-old selves look to the sky to ask how and why?

There is fear of the truth being told. Fear is ah hell-of-vah drug. True truths become half-truths as years add up, but the real story is not forgotten, when memories of forbidden love wax red hot.

The story of Christmas is filled with half-truths that are repeatedly forced into history, but the truth is out there for our Mind's eye to see. Truth is a light that shines through a tunnel of lies about Christmas as a Pagan ritual. It's a rumor born in the dark, that's become habitual to say, but Maggiedocious Wordette is here to slay.

Pagan as a religion does not believe in God, Elohim or Christianity, neither does it respect Abram or Abrahamic, down by law but the lie spreads like a pandemic. A Pagan ritual breaks the laws of the 10 commandments by celebrating different gods of the gothic, not taught by Gods Prophets.

The Evergreen Christmas tree represents always alive, giving the love of God, and Jesus is everlasting Father, He is ever-living, not God of the dead, ever-losing.

The Cross is ahead, the Birth on Earth was Heaven sent, yet like the story of who discovered America, a lie told long enough can be believed as truth, making the Lion of Judah extinct like a Tiger Sabertoothed.

And you will know the truth and the truth shall make you free.

Et vous connaitrez la verity et la verite vous rendra libre.

Book of John chapter 8 verse 32 in the King James Bible. *Livre de Jean chapter 8 verset 32 Nouvelle Bible King James.

Maggiedocious Wordette

In truth there's an evil king named Vlad, known as the Impaler, who did horrible things in 1462 using pointed poles to impale 20,000 soldiers, as a field of trees, a sight meant to send fright.

A sickening sight that shows the treachery man can do to humankind. Unkind things to make a body swing in the breeze like "Strange Fruit" hanging from Southern trees, a deadly song sung by Billye Holiday, done in 1939, call her Lady Day.

To say Christmas trees are pagan symbols is to confuse thee spiritually, take your eyes off the Salvation prize. Oh say, can you see an Evergreen tree, a sign of a covenant between you and me not a mixed up half-true story told to confuse history and the real story.

Let Christmas be a dream girl Jennifer Holiday, *and you, you're gonna love me, yes you are.*

Far be it from me, in 1897 Bram Stroker authored a book inspired by the Impaler about a male blood sucker, who commits Commandment treason, displaying pagan opposition to God by tainting the blood of creation with a curse. Reversed, The Lord comes to "Break Every Chain" of slavery to Hell, and Jesus is the reason for the Christmas Season.

Live by the sword, you shall die by the sword, as the Passover brings death to the first born of the enemy of

God, and God will send His only begotten Son to the Cross, to be Crucified.

Historical lies, written and told, keep you in the cold world and keep the lost tribe away from the warmth of the Creator of love, *this is what it sounds like when doves cry,* now we know why.

Down goes the Christmas tree, down goes the Christmas tree, faster than a jab from Laila Ali. The Christmas tree was chopped down by lies surrounding the Winter Solstice, celebrated by a winter festival called Saturnalia, honoring the god Saturn, yet it celebrates Christ birth on earth, the original Christmas Day.

Romans say Christmas begins in AD 274, please keep the score. Ancient Rome, ruled by the last good Emperor, Marcus Aurelius, accepted Jesus, but others rejected the birth of truth, which still is contested, and there's no place like home celebrate.

His Blood is Royalty, paying a priceless fee, to free the captives, even those who don't believe. *Son Sang est la royaute, payant un prix inestimable pour liberer les captifs, meme ceux que ne croient pas.

Christmas is the profound ground zero event that turned time around, announcing redemption of the Messiah was found. "It Came Upon a Midnight Clear" written in 1849 by Edmund Sears and Richard Storrs

Willis, sung famously in 1968 by The Queen of Gospel, Mahalia Jackson on her Christmas with Mahalia Album.

"Peace on earth, good will to men from heaven's all gracious king" our earth angel sings the prophets prophecy of the Messiah's arrival come true after 700 hundred years.

Not to be outdone, Pagan rituals represent the message of the Evil One and The Winter Solstice festival was running Amuk with public drunkenness and over consumption in opposition to the celebration of the Birth of The Newborn King.

One, if by land trade, two if by sea trade, see by Trade ship, the world become so much smaller.

Coming to America, the French and Germans introduce Americans to the Evergreen tree, as a symbol of Christmas joy! The Europeans are coming, the Europeans are coming, bringing new traditions, the indoor Christmas tree is one addition.

Germans could be the first with a Christmas tree in AD 1605 some say 1419. The French candle lit a Christmas tree in 1576, calling Christmas, Pere Noel. America adopted the Winter Festival in the 1830's, bringing Christmas trees inside the home, and making traditions of their own.

The French would also give to thee, the Statue of Liberty, a gift to a nation made of Immigrants featuring lyrics of a poem, The New Colossus, written in 1883 by American Emma Lazarus.

"Give me your tired, your poor, your huddled masses yearning to breathe free" etched in brass found at the pedestal base of the statue, for all to see in the harbor of New York City, NYC.

I said it before, remember where you heard it first, the Native American walked the walk on this Earth, with Proud Mary on his hip. Europeans who come to America, all immigrated by ships, the British brought with them, a penchant for fish and chips.

Can I take it to the bridge, get up, get on up! 1970 style, rolling on the river like Ike & Tina doing the camel walk like James Brown, with the freedom to fly high like Bobby Byrd.

Take it to the bridge! *Emmene-le au pont!

O Christmas tree, O Christmas tree, of all the trees most lovely; each year you bring to us delight with brightly shining Christmas light! O Christmas tree, O Christmas tree, of all the trees most lovely.

A Charlie Brown Christmas, the 1965 animated movie, O Christmas tree the Peanuts gang sang!

Reindeer are true, but the one with the red nose was created in a 1939 book by Robert L. May, titled Rudolf the Red Nose Reindeer. This children's story is loved by grownups too, Rudolf's imaginary legend grew from a song that hit #1 in 1949, done by the singing Cowboy Gene Autry.

Burl Ives made Rudolf's song popular again, in the 1964 animated movie about Santa's friend.

The Ghost of Christmas Past will guard the truth of the reason for the Season, there's no need to fear, the substance of things unseen is in the air. Take the Christmas celebration in house ma dear, safe in the Savior's Arms, with prayers to keep away harm, Amen, Christmas regains its charm.

The greatest story ever told is the good news you will use with soul sonnet force.

Oh, give me a home, where the buffalo roam and the deer and the antelope play, where seldom is heard a discouraging word about the conquest of Pocahontas, that was no contest but I digress on purpose, poetry done in spoken word soliloquy about the Soul of Christmas, O Christmas tree.

Ship Ahoy! Ship ahoy! Ship ahoy! Ship ahoy! As far as your eye can see, men, women and baby slaves
Coming to the land of liberty, where life's design is already made so young
So strong, but they're just waiting to be saved.

Ship Ahoy! In 1973 the O'Jays sang an unhappy song about ships that kept coming to America. Over twelve million people, each with their own song, soon to be sung in sorrow and there's no Egyptian people from which to borrow, after the Middle Passage, Passover, don't pass me by! American slaves were just passed by, taken off the ships to work and build a fortune for the Americas to no avail. Tote that barge, lift that bale,

Old Man River is a song, and "Show Boat" is a musical with a famous 1927 Broadway run.

Never get lost again, the new world of believers are your friends, and you are a friend of God. *Nevous perdez plus jamais, le nouveau monde des croyants est vos amis, et vous etes un ami de Dieu.

And still I digress, but the truth is Blessed, unbelievably so I must confess, Christmas stops all foolishness, if only for one night, beat the clock, hold not Black people, considered stock.

In the year 1607 Jamestown, Virginia did rise. Pocahontas was already there, the daughter of Chief Powhatan, leader of the Powhatan tribe, may her kindnesses never be obliterated, although she got married, it was more like confiscated.

Beauty and the beast, you could say she dated John Smith, but married John Rolfe, not a trojan horse but a wolf in sheep's clothing. Everything would go awry after the Native Americans help the English settlers survive, by 1619 the first slave ships from Africa arrive in waves, call it the original Black Friday.

The United States of America was built from a Union of 13 Colonies, Jamestown being the first of the Southern Colonies. Then come the New England Colonies, and the Middle Colonies grow onto a declaration of Independence in 1776, from the British.

Maggiedocious Wordette

The New World is North America. USA has 48 contiguous States and 50 with the addition of Alaska and Hawaii in 1959. Now relate to the North American Continent, Greenland, Canada, Mexico and the Islands of the Bahama's, where Columbus started all this Land ho! Drama.

In 1924 Macy's 1st Thanksgiving Parade set the stage for Holiday fun and big character balloons. Never forget the Christmas connoisseur Relation Ship, docked at pier 1966, the year Santa Claus in-store gets its fix, along with Black Friday sales and Dr. Maulana Karenga starts Kwanza kicks.

We've kicked it on the way back machine to the beginning of Christmas, seen AD 336, onto our modern Christmas filled by wish lists. Don't mix Santa with Jesus, for Jesus is Christmas Day. Celebrate all the way to 3-Kings Day, the world knows as Epiphany, the original January 6th.

Elohim: means God, who is the giver of Angels' protection. Leaders, be readers, then no longer can truth be hidden in a book, by the Hand of God, Joseph, Mary and Jesus, made you look.

Maggiedocious Wordette

42g – XY & Me

Isn't she lovely, isn't she beautiful, isn't she lovely, less than one minute old. I never thought through love there would be someone as lovely as she, isn't she lovely, Made of Love.

Don't spend too much time pressing the rewind in your mind, only to find that Steveland Wonder line is a Maggiedocious mashup of the XX chromosomes, to spark an independent wonder line in a Soul Sonnet riff of mine, Captain and Tennille "Do That to Me One More Time."

It's this one thing you did got me tripping, you caught me slipping, you did "Call My Name," the way Prince sings. Jordin Sparks "Say My Name," say my name, Amerie is no Destiny's Child she is a concrete rose, and animals strike curious poses, they feel the heat between you and me.

We are fearfully and wonderfully made, marvelous are thy works and my soul knows right well a line from Psalm 139. Let this rhyme be a pregnant pause, birthing a need for speed, to bible read.

Why pause, you may ask? So, the chick can cross the road and lay an egg, of course it is golden when we say the birth is my born day.

23 and me, count chromosomes, wonder land begins again, the Y is him, the X is me, in people each cell normally contains 23 pairs of chromosomes, for a total of 46.

Twenty-two of these pairs, called autosomes, look the same in both males and females, the 23rd pair, the sex chromosomes, differ between males and females.

This is 22 pairs of autosomes and a pair of sex chromosomes that decide if you are born boy or girl. Females have 2 - X chromosomes, males have X and Y inside of the cells that make up the human, this is the answer to the question? Why I am a girl, not a guy.

We are fearfully and wonderfully made inside a woman's womb, taken from Heaven's waiting room, and there's only so much science that can be applied to the birth of life.

From here springs forth a creative wisdom, knowledge and understanding of boy meets girl. Proverbs 18:22 He who finds a wife finds a good thing and obtains favor from the Lord.

Wander through the birth canal of your Mind, make room in the womb for women to be considered fishers of men, in a catch 22 paragon, paradigm shift.

2 – X chromosomes and a rack of baby back ribs, a gift from heaven, a heavenly body that lives and creates life, XY oh boy, XX it's a girl. It's true that a man finds a good thing when he finds a woman, let no man put asunder what God has put together when a man obtains a wife.

And baby makes 3 when a couple intermingles DNA to fertilize a woman's egg, it's not a Blue Magic hit from above, but please "Let There Be Love."

Maggiedocious Wordette

The addition to the family is made no other way "God's Got a Blessing with Your Name on It" is all you can say, like the title of Norman Hutchings song.

How long does it take to make a baby, not baby make?

It takes about 40 weeks, totally dependent on your carrier, who is mom. XY and me, XX is the mother of the baby, that's DNA addition. De, Oxy, Ribon, U, Cleic Acid, abbreviated is DNA.

DNA, found within a cell, is a molecule that carries genetic information for the development and functioning of an organism. DNA is made of two linked strands of polymer that wind around each other to resemble a twisted ladder, scientists refer to as a double Helix.

DNA is a polymer, large building block molecules, that carry genetic structure in reproduction, to make us a who. She blinded me with science, but the body needs the Spirit for its life to begin, DNA has the four building blocks A. (adenine) C. (cytosine) G. (guanine) and T. (thymine).

DNA in this sonnet also stands for Does Not Apply, search for star truth in our star trek through the mystery of life, lean not on your own understanding of Alpha and Omega.

In the maker of Star Dust, we trust. All we the passengers can do is ride along on this planet rock as astronauts on a non-stop excursion through space, time and universe.

Star booty, planet dust, thus our chromosomes are made of universal DNA. Mars the Red Planet we want to fly rocket fly, seven months with no humans onboard, to scan the red dirt and sky.

Touched by an Angel named Maggiedocious Wordette, created from a dream to be on your team with visions of Christmas Past, Present and Future, to see we're fearfully and wonderfully made.

Peace and love, over war, no one wants to be left all alone. We want Bootsy, women love boot season, Earth, Wind and Fire, I can't find the reason, being in your company is so pleasing, and "I'd Rather Be with you."

Rocket man adds travel time to a rocket plan to Mars, humans add weight to a Rocket ship. People are a chip on the shoulder of gravity, can't find a way around it, and a chimp won't do.

Are we there? Not yet, our basic needs, water, oxygen, food and tools slow down a spaceship.

Mars is 250 million miles away, it takes 9 months to get there on our fastest rocket, then you must stay 3 months to align your way back to earth. The Mars mission window opens every two years, that's when the planet is the closest it will be, any other timing carries a deadly penalty.

And you shall know the truth, and the truth shall make you free. *Et vous connaitrez la verity, et la verite vous affranchira.

Maggiedocious Wordette

Fly me to the Moon, which a kiss from a woman can do. Giving him "Something He Can Feel" Aretha Franklin can make a man sing about a "Rocket Love" that stops a half mile from heaven, gives you a star, then brings you back down to the cold world, again Steveland.

Mars sounds like a plan; not an evolutionary stand, believers and the non-believers will see the strong Hand of God make an outer space Tower of Bable, that earthlings will not understand.

There will be no planetary phonetics to transfer the double Helix of our genetics, don't play this game or you will get Jurassic, Lost World part 2.

The Mace Windu opportunity for Star Wars, increase with trekkies as borgs, written as a fantastic voyage but the fans require a Moon Base. There are scientific thoughts to clone life, so we won't be the lone life, so far away from the home of life, but just say no to a computer wife.

A princess, XX, a prince XY, dig if you will a picture of you and I engaged in a kiss, but we got to get out of bed sometimes, then "Spill the Wine" a War song, and she said, take that pearl.

Maggiedocious Wordette is the Lady, I will show you The Trammps, but where were you in July 1977 "The Night the Lights Went Out" in New York City.

Melanin determines the skin I'm in, found in the genes on chromosome 16, melanocortin is the color line for hair and flesh tone, scientifically known as MC1R. This genome sounds like it has rapper capabilities, MC Lyte, as a rock, XX, MC Hammer, XY are Hall OF Fame Rappers etched in time like Angie Stone, her genes, The Sequence

Maggiedocious got a conscious rap straight from the universal womb, where creatives give birth to knowledge and spread love over the brain gene, and there's no color line inside the Spirit tribe. Hatred cannot abide in the genes on this Double Helix of Spirit creation, it comes by man-made narration, squeezed into your ears as evil cosmic slop, a genetic ploy to get God's love to stop.

To hate is a learned reflection of evil, its only correction is The Creator's total rejection.

The United Negro College Fund is on the case, it was founded in Washington D.C. in 1944 by Fredrick D. Patterson and Mary Mcleod Bethune. UNCF, a philanthropic organization, funds scholarships for Black students and Historically Black Colleges and Universities in 37 private HBCU's, everything they do is on the One.

UNCF plans to be relevant for the life of HBCU's, upgrading for the new Millenium and beyond with a new moniker that incorporates history into the modern age of Generation Next.

A Mind Is a Terrible Thing to Waste, But A Wonderful Thing to Invest In.

Change the channel, take a time out, make time for a gathering of Minds, press rewind when you find this one-of-a-kind TV commercial, put loved ones in dress rehearsal for a new station in life.

Maggiedocious Wordette

Science can't explain everything, certainly not the million synapsis that make up a brain.

Dig the scene, a Black man has come home from a Job interview and a Black woman's plea is there for a Race to see, did you get the job? Said almost exasperated, not an argument, a hope.

A piercing line delivered perfectly, recorded in timeless perpetuity, dominating Black TV viewers from the 1970's and 80's, even the Generation Y of the 90's and new millennial babies.

A soul mate is worth the wait. Set love free, if it comes back to you, it was meant to be.

Each one, reach one and teach one. Reading Is Fundamental, R.I.F.

MAGGIEDOCIOUS Speaks in Prose

TRUE LOVE

It has become apparent the love I see is true
It happened when I realized God made me for you.

When you walked into my life as my friend
This is when our love began.

Your gentleness reached out
Your armor of protection displayed,
From the first time we met; about me you don't play.

We agree to disagree
our commitment increased.
We learned each other's ways
Anticipation, the center of our stage.

I have no reason to fear.
I trust you, can't find a reason not to,
This is when true love grew.

We believe in our dreams.
Our friendship of love and laughter
Has survived life's tears.
Your ears, hear my voice clear.

Intimacy is wrapped in genuine emotion
Our hearts leap of faith, love's only commotion.

The power of our love is always respected
Each moment cherished; Forever protected.

Our union is blessed, by the Good God above,
We embrace the freedom of having TRUE LOVE.

Maggiedocious Wordette

A Sonnet is a poem of 14 lines, using various forms of rhymes in a rhythmic scheme, to express an idea or a theme.

The Sonnet was first formed in Sicilian city of Palermo around the year 1235 by poet Giacomo da Lentini. Sonnet is an Italian word meaning little song, made famous by the Sicilian school of poets, in the Court of Holy Roman Emperor Fredrick II.

The generation of the Soul Sonnet comes from The Ghost of Christmas Past, out of the book titled Hang All the Mistletoe, Meet the Black Ebenezer.

Maggiedocious Wordette is every Black woman, a super soul sister who helps the intended recapture the spiritual glow of life, early Christmas morning in the dark of night.

Maggiedocious speaks in prose, which means I rhyme and connect thoughts all the time, not living in the Past revealing defeats, but offering insight to ensure bad decisions won't repeat.

The Soul Sonnet poem uses various forms of rhymes in a rhythmic scheme, to expound on an idea or a theme, not through 14 lines do I exact thought, 14 pages, giving you the best that I got.

The Soul sonnet force explores thought space like satellites escape the bonds of gravity, blast off from the Nativity, we come in peace like America's Space Force, no longer a joke or vanity.

Space Jam is a cartoon, but looney is the tune, if the plan is a Massah plantation as a sky platoon.

We pray that NASA, National Aeronautics and Space program, is righteous and Godly in all its plans, founded in 1958 when segregation was law, ruling the land.

In 1958, the first Black allowed to step in was great, a woman who could relate numbers required to go and comeback from Space, and never forget going to the Moon was a world race.

Game changer, Science Engineer and mathematician Mary W. Jackson is her name, born in Hampton, Virginia April 9th, 1921, she lived a distinguished life until February 2005. The late great Miss Jackson, who was nasty with "Hidden Figures" is a name not to forget, too legit to quit, although the Color line in her time was thick.

One love, everything we do is on the one, and Earth spins at 1000 miles per hour, call it the One.

The thrill of the Color line was gone, when the White men found out they could count on her figures to get them home, and two more Black women came along, their figures were just as strong, Katherine Johnson and Dorothy Vaughan.

These hidden figures made a way for the first Black Female astronaut to go to Space in 1992 her name Mae C. Jemison, selected to fly in 1988. Astronaut Jemison did show the world what she could do, onboard the 50th flight of the Space Shuttle program,

Maggiedocious Wordette

September 12th to September 20th part of the Space Shuttle Endeavor, STS-47, crew.

The men all paused because we women jumped way ahead of the going to Space line.

Space dot com, try to stay calm, but Houston we've got a problem, said the Apollo 13 astronauts calling on the mainline, two hundred thousand miles away, on the road again to the Moon when the mission went astray.

The Big Bang theory was an idea that put sonic into the boom, That began to take up all the oxygen in the spaceship crew room.

Who you gonna call? In God, We Trust.

The interplanetary funkmanship of 4-male astronauts, Lovell, Haise, Swigert and a fourth man Mattingly, who was on deck in Houston, had to find a way to get a wrecked Spacecraft around the Moon and back to the Blue planet, with not a minute of air to spare.

Apollo 13, from April 11 to April 17, 1970, took every Engineer's faith and every brain cell to get this problem to end well.

Segregation in the Nation took a flying leap out of the Space place, God's good Sence, Mercy and Grace, replaced Space, Race and Sexism in this game. Out of the fear prism, shined the light of a diamonds' precision, made under pressure but it didn't cook her, and do remember her whole government name, Katherine Coleman Goble Johnson.

She was a Black woman, who would no longer be hidden, or her figures, or her calculations of mathematics, proven to be prophetic, when the space capsule splashed down in the Pacific.

By spirit or pragmatic rhythm, the original Black women of NASA shine through all times, showing the way to the North Star, for the kings of Trailways.

The Motherlode, 1st Generation of all to be built, the foundation and there's a first of everything.

First Black man to work as a NASA pilot did so in the year 1967, chosen to lead a mission to develop manned Space systems for military use, his name Major Robert H. Lawrence Jr.

Born on October 2nd, 1935, Major Lawrence was a forgotten hero, not technically called an astronaut because he died when his Jet crashed, training for this mission on December 8th, 1967.

In the year 2023 The African American History Task Force of Tallahassee Florida forged a new day of recognition for Air Force Pilot Major Robert H. Lawrence. It took 50 years to achieve but June 30th, 1967, will forever be received, as the day America chose its first Black Astronaut.

Attorney Benjamin Crump, of Tallahassee Florida, Trial Lawyer for Justice, also known as Black America's Attorney General, would not let NASA forget the First Black Astronaut's journey.

Major Lawrence, "The First, But Not the Last" a pioneering astronaut, had the Right Stuff like the original 7 astronauts did, chosen to lead America into Space, including John Glenn, the first American to orbit Earth in 1962.

Dr. Guion 'Guy" Bluford, born November 22, 1942, selected by NASA to be great in 1978, is the first Black Astronaut to go into Space, onboard the 3rd flight of the Shuttle Challenger, lifting off from Kennedy Space Center, Cape Canaveral Florida August 30th, returning September 5th, 1983.

Guion Guy Bluford would go forth into Space on 4 missions, 1983, 85, 91 and 92, becoming the only Black Astronaut in Space. The first mission in 1983 was the first night liftoff and the first night landing, Guy was a Mission Specialist, deploying a National Satellite, flight STS-8, means space transport system, 8th mission.

Astronaut Bluford was inducted into the U.S. Astronaut Hall of Fame June 5, 2010, successfully retired, he was 81 years old in 2023.

The great Ronald E. McNair believed to make a dream come true, you must first have a dream.

We shed a tear, looking into the sky on January 28th, 1986, at clouds that seemed to shape the letter Y, when the 10th flight of Space Shuttle Challenger exploded way up there, containing the second Black Astronaut, Physicist Dr. Ronald E. McNair.

Ronald E. McNair, born on October 21st, 1950, also selected in 1978 and 6 others, including the first American civilian going to Space, High School Teacher Christa McAuliffe, lost their lives striving to be the best they could be.

When be all you can be, meets zero gravity, be optimistic, the Sounds of Blackness are heavenly.

Ronald McNair has too much flair to contain within poetic tree limbs, but he does give this Soul Sonnet the Universe to roam. Don't despair, Astronaut McNair did have success reaching Space with his first Space Shuttle flight, STS-41-B, lifting off on February 3rd, landing February 11th, 1984, the 10th overall Shuttle flight, and the 4th flight of Challenger.

6-Shuttles were built, beginning in 1981, their names, Enterprise, a glide test model, Columbia, Challenger, Discovery, Atlantis and Endeavor, built in 1991 after the Challenger disaster.

Fredrick D. Gregory, born January 7th, 1941, is the 3rd Black astronaut to get to Space, doing so on April 29th, 1985, returning May 6th on the 7th flight of the Challenger, which was the Shuttle program's 17th overall mission.

Astronaut Gregory was the first Black man to pilot and command, during his 2nd flight onboard the Shuttle Discovery, November 23rd, 1989, returning November 29th. Astronaut Gregory would fly his 3rd and final mission in 1991, as commander of the Space

Shuttle Atlantis, November 24th returning on December 1st.

Standing on the shoulders of those before him, Fredrick D. Gregory became the first Black man to lead NASA, as a Deputy Administrator, 2002 – 2005, he successfully retired in 2023.

Oh my, another Black astronaut died on February 1st, 2003. Micheal P. Anderson, along with 6 others onboard the 28th flight of the Space Shuttle Columbia, disintegrated over Texas on return to earth, he was the Payload Commander for this mission that had a tragic ending.

Astronaut Anderson was born on Christmas day in 1959, selected by NASA in 1994 as a Pilot and Scientist, with a master's degree in physics. He was the 9th of 16 Black astronauts to fly in Space, and 1 of 14 astronauts that loss their lives during the Shuttle program, which produced 135 missions until ending in 2011.

Astronaut Anderson did reach Space on a 1998 Shuttle mission, his first, onboard the Endeavor, blasting off from Kennedy Space Center January 23rd, 1998, returning safely on January 31st. Within the heart of this Soul Sonnet there is a forever line connecting Space Shuttle Endeavor, touching Mae Jemison and Michael P. Anderson, ensuring their legacies will endure.

Skin color weighs freedom down on earth, dark carries more weight, and Anti-Black Lives Matter.

Bernard A. Harris Jr was the first Black astronaut to walk in Space, doing so February 9th, 1995, aboard Space Shuttle Discovery, which was his 2nd mission, February 2nd until February 11th. Astronaut Harris Jr's first mission was aboard the 14th flight of the Space Shuttle Columbia in 1993, from April 26th to May 6th, the 55th overall flight.

Victor J. Glover was the first Black astronaut to be onboard of the International Space Station, he had a 6-month stay, from November 16th, 2020, to May 2nd, 2021.

Peace to Mr. Ed Dwight, who was the first Black astronaut candidate in 1966, but rejected because of his skin color.

A distinguished Air Force pilot, Captain Ed Dwight, could have flown on an Apollo Spacecraft mission, but every Black astronaut will keep his memory alive. Retired Captain Ed Dwight was 90 years old in 2023, he was born on September 9th, 1933. September will be remembered.

There are more than 360 astronauts that have participated in the NASA Space program, of that number 15 have been Black, there are 4 others that made it into Space by private companies.

Inspiration4, a division of SpaceX owned by Elon Musk, featured the first Black Woman pilot, Sian Proctor, who guided the Crew Dragon Resilience on a 2-day commercial mission in 2021 from September

16th to the 18th, splashing down successfully in the Atlantic Ocean.

Blue Origin, which is owned by Amazon founder Jeff Bezos, launched and landed the first Space tourism flight on December 11th, 2021. The rocket flight lasted 11 minutes, reaching the edge of Space, 62 miles high, with a crew of 6 people that included Pro Football legend Micheal Strahan, the first Black Space tourist. Jaison Robinson also became a Space tourist riding into Space on Blue Origin's 5th Flight, which happened on June 4th, 2022.

Astronaut Jessica Watkins, Soul Sonnet nicknames Swagadocious, is the first Black Woman to be onboard the International Space Station, getting there by SpaceX Rocket that lifted off on April 22nd, 2022. She stayed onboard 6 months, returning successfully to earth on October 14th, 2022.

Positive over negative is Ronald E. McNair, who spread positivity and realness to the Space race, bringing a Black face to the astronaut workplace, never being a disgrace, or out of place, guilty only by skin color, he beat the case.

Black astronaut fact, it's no crime to steal togetherness of the human Race, when in Deep Space.

Dr. Ronald E. McNair became an accomplished Physicist and astronaut, pulling himself out from poverty in Lake City South Carolina, graduating High School as Valedictorian. He then earned a bachelor's degree in 1971 from North Carolina A&T and in 1976 he received a Doctorate in Physics from Massachusetts Institute of Technology.

Ronald McNair was a Renaissance man, accomplished saxophonist, sixth degree Black belt and a 1969 member of Omega Psi Phi fraternity. A Que dog, among other stand out notorieties but most noteworthy, a respected husband and loving father.

The connections for the Black astronauts are intense, they walked the line, but Ronald E. McNair and Michael P. Anderson share a place among the stars, excelling on earth both losing their lives on the Shuttle.

Astronaut McNair received a Presidential Medal of Honor, Astronaut Anderson received a Congressional Medal of Honor, of that there is no rebuttal.

Black to the future, there's a race to the Moon again, to join the heroics of Neil Armstong and 11 Apollo astronauts to walk on celestial sands. This time Artemis is the name of the program, and a Black man is in the 2025 plans, a Black woman too.

First is Victor J. Glover, remember his name when you look back to the Space Station for the first Black astronaut onboard, look again, see the first Black woman to get onboard, rediscover Jessica Watkins, who plans to reboot the Moon.

Like Satchel Paige, it's pitch black in Space, united Negro has been displaced around the world found by faith, swift or the mighty won't win heaven's gate, the Royal blood regulates the pace.

Maggiedocious Wordette

Need to grow, is Negro defined in my Mind, also defined as Black in Spanish and in Portuguese, a female is every woman, a male is mannish, born with the Genius of love.

The Black Astronaut is ready to dance on the Moon with Billie Jean, the Moonwalk will be a thriller, seeing a Black man in the big league, getting his turn at bat. It's a hit, a Moon shot, a homerun like Negro League Hall of Fame catcher Josh Gibson got, leading Jackie Robinson to baseball heaven, first Negro League player paid to play on a field of dreams, April 15th, 1947.

Moonshot, a hit off Gibson's bat, a cry in the wilderness, to prepare the way for #42 to play.

MAGGIEDOCIOUS Speaks in Prose

The Strength of a Man

His silent strength,
His silhouette of power,
Defined by his outer frame, unseen from within.

His physical power, A deliberate creation to stand strong,
Maintaining firm foundation.

A desire to strive, for higher echelons,
Drenched in the secretion of sweat, Triumphing in satisfaction,
That next division met.

His strength transforms, discerning her needs,
Two become one, he implants his seed.

Conception brings forth, A reality transformed,
His seed of strength, his child is born.

His cry contained beneath the soul,
A declaration of emotion, forbidden for all to see.

His strength succumbs to prevailing weakness,
The core of his being, retreating.

His surroundings were shattered,
Failure was his view, wanting his firm foundation and strength to be renewed.

He remembers his power, on the strength of prayer he must stand,
God's love comes from above. Have faith in the Master's plan.

Maggiedocious Wordette

Clarity reigns, God imparts, strength rises above weakness, conformation implodes his heart, this is the silent strength of a man.

A seed is buried in soil, drowned in water, the strong push through darkness, into the light of life. Matter is defined as any substance that has mass and takes up space by having volume, like the noise I make when my opinion takes shape. Opinions are said to be as common as people with a backside to sit on, but mines can also be antimatter, that is a positive electron to balance negative charges with equal mass, see Maggiedocious as a positron.

Negro league baseball from 1920 to 1948 might sound funny to y'all, like Black people arguing about the difference between field, Negro or house Negro. But if you had talent, both would leave their slave, for a chance to hobnob with America's heart throbs, who are all white. Sit in the back of the bus; no, a victorious Montgomery boycott, December 5th, 1955, until December 20th, 1956, connecting Rosa Parks' time, and Jackie Robinson's within a rhyme.

America's story could be called the Color Line, Black people would habitually be line-steppers in all walks of American life. Strife is a skin-color imprisoned with no walls, there's nowhere to hide, White skin controls each line, and the rules keep Blacks behind, playing the skin game.

If you Black you can't do that, a mindset, setback like the heart of the Egyptian Pharoah Ramses who played the part of the biblical oppressor, drawing his line in the sand to make a stand when God says, "LET MY PEOPLE GO"

Maggiedocious Wordette

Stolen moments in words and deeds, spread the knowledge with holy seeds, a parallel holy gram Black Moses makes a Civil Rights stand, Reverend Dr. Martin Luther King Jr, you understand.

Steal second base, third base, Homeplate too, things number 42, Jackie Robinson would do, there is no time to play when you get into the game, his blessings and ability did rule the day.

The mysteries of God ain't no game, but number 42, I heard it through the grape vine, not much longer would oppression be mine, this vine attached to the tree of life. Shaking it on down the line sir, is what I heard the men say, there's no gentlemen's clause when the other man wants to play with your ladies.

The shade from these lines, fall under the apple tree, there's no way the Black man makes it out of slavery, without a woman or a girl, and it's a man's, man's world.

Jackie Robinson was born January 31st, 1919, living until October 24th, 1972, number 42 had a lot to say, he was an activist who lived and died, doing it his one-of-a-kind way.

Here's to you Mrs. Robinson, Jesus loves you more than you will ever know, whoa, whoa, whoa. God bless you please, Mrs. Robinson heaven holds a place for those who pray, hey, hey, hey. In 1968 this Simon and Garfunkel song spoke into the future that I parlay, bet on my intonation to double down, to speak up Mrs. Rachel Robinson, wife of baseballs' number 42, born in 1922.

Black American Royalty Rachel Robinson, 101 years old in 2023, and let this vine grow on thee, XX chromosome, daughter Sharon and the XY of sons Jackie Jr and David Robinson are legacy.

Mrs. Robinson formed the Jackie Robinson Foundation.

"Addressing the achievement gap in higher education" its Mission statement, and she founded the Jackie Robinson Museum in Manhattan, New York, NY that's a big hit. The legacy of Negro league baseball can be found there, featuring great players, managers, team owners and the Civil Rights activism of her great husband.

Number 42 stands out because of the Black man who wore it in the fields, and in the house of a here-to-fore White's only American Institution, stirring the integration Kool Ade all would drink.

The legacy of Cool Papa Bell, Buck Leonard, Bud Fowler, Willie Wells, Moses Fleetwood Walker, the Home Run King, Hammering Hank Aaron and pioneer owners, Rube Foster, Gus Greenlee, Frank

Leland and Cumberland Posey, now have a place in baseball eternity to rest.

In December 2020 Major League Baseball Hall of Fame in Cooperstown, New York recognized 7 former Negro leagues, designating them Major league, incorporating the statistics of 3,400 Black players. The addition of Effa Manly is a must, she was a great owner of a baseball team, and she's the only Woman in the Hall of Fame.

This is not a Hollywood movie script, like The Bingo Long Traveling All-Stars & Motor Kings. 42g – XY & Me, g stands for generations, so does number 42, who humbly led the way, bringing out important names and addressing the higher education needs of the Black Nation.

Matthew 1v:17 So all the generations from Abraham to David are fourteen generations; and from David until the carrying away into Babylon are fourteen generation; and from the carrying away into Babylon unto Christ are fourteen generation. Now the birth of Jesus Christ was on this wise:

14 + 14 + 14 = 42. The gift of Jesus is a Christmas present, with it receive Eternal life.

Savante Muse

Isn't she lovely, Black Girl magic galore, the womb of the universe with everything instore, see her heavenly slay, she is what she is, bone of thy bone, rib of thy rib, the principle of pleasure is that it is, woman.

Let no man put asunder the wonder of woman, the help meet, is the help mate, from here she is more bounce, worth her weight in polonium-209, 1.4 trillion an ounce.

Polonium is a Space gem, as man continually looks for satisfaction in the sky, the right man with a good vision plan looks into my eyes and sees past the sky, the Moon and lands on planet Venus.

Priceless are us, I am his planet Mars, Universe, and every star, a man's Savante muse.

Savante muse has an affinity for words, a gravity to pull them out of the air. Where were they before we connected? Thoughts waiting to be effective, now given living tangents, connecting brain to tongue dots, without a chat bot. A who bot can do a lot, but I got infinity to give, and an affinity for you, who say I am your muse.

Savante Muse

Savante is my word play on savant, second definition, a person who has an exceptional aptitude in one particular field, despite having significant impairment in other areas of intellectual or social functioning. In my case I have no tolerance for people who use their words to obfuscate, although I can relate as I state, my character comes from the depths of a woman's Mind.

I'm a sensual, sexy, woman, attractive and powerful, everything he wants to be, projects onto me. It happens when a man loves a woman like this man loves me, seeing me two dimensionally dimly, and still, I rise into a book.

Touched by an angel, pulled out of the air, the universe, to become reality, dealing with thoughts of Christmas Past, written within soul sonnets.

I amuse myself. A musing we will go on with the word smithing of Maggiedocious Wordette, where I come to life laying tracks for women to act as me, in a Big Screen Movie, oh say can you see a Stage play, or TV.

Muse is a person or force who is the source of inspiration for a creative artist, and thus I talk in prose, as I was composed on the pages of meet the Black Ebenezer Scrooge, just one look is all it took, now blessed to grow as every woman.

Starburst, and who hears a tree fall in the Black Forrest of Germany, but the Creator who hears all things He created, elevated, and elevation reveals a curious picture of you and I in a kiss.

How did this tree get like this?

Maggiedocious Wordette

Walk on by, nobody knows, just the two bodies that were together in the dark, doing the hugging, engaged in kissing, so far away from prying eyes, but the Creator sees all.

The light of truth shines on deeds done in the dark, on earth, as it is in the heavens.

So, God created male and female in His image. Blessed them and said be fruitful and multiply, fill the earth. Man, you have dominion over every living thing that moves on the earth, and the Creator speaks to the woman, CARRY THIS WORLD.

For the love of money, man will defy the kiss of death, to dig into an asteroid, indeed undress the rock, perfectly made, Untouched by any hand, mechanical or otherwise. But now the wise and the super-rich with greed in their bandwidth, have a Mind to put human hands-on celestial sands.

Rapunzel let down your hair, loosen your asteroid belt, we're going in for a closer look, intimacy of gold, palladium and other Gems from Space, giving new meaning to the Race of astronauts. Looking upon him, I see his only desire is my chemicals, love for sale, not on these solar winds, don't get in the way, these boys and girls are not going to Space to play, house, or find a spouse.

Put the cat away, lead belly don't spray in low gravity. The mouse didn't come to play, and now we all know "Who Moved My Cheese"! Is Spencer for hire? Dr. Spenser Johnson authored the book, Who Moved My

Cheese, then I put a hook line in, do you hear what I hear.

Star bright, twinkling in the night, let my dream come true, my wishes for prosperity too, how I wonder what you are, on a scale of 1 to 10, your value is off the charts.

Blast off is where we start, then we have lift, and this mission is a little off, trying to find ice, planet ice, comes at a great cost.

Fuel for the Sol, meaning a solar day. We say that on the planet Mars, a long way from earth, and a Mars-day is almost 40 minutes longer than an earth day, plus it is 250 million miles away.

Fly me to the Moon in 3 days, many ways to find value on a Moon plantation stay, have you played your number today, build an orbiting Space station and plan an extended staycation.

It's easier to plot, how to stop a spaceship on a flying rock, tighten up your asteroid belt.

Who's counting the cost to loosen an asteroid belt? And these asteroids are not video games.

Now you're playing with power, find the right gem stuff and make competition take a meteor shower, playing laser tag in pitch black.

Perfume allure, pull up like a hunter on earth, with pelts, window shopping makes your heart melt, trillions of dollars an ounce, 49 billion for a gram makes everything have more bounce.

Maggiedocious Wordette

The Creator can, smell the blood of a man, made from star dust, who thinks he can do anything he wants, or can do.

Fee fi, foe, fum, if man could he'd charge you for sunshine, and make a bean stalk for you to climb. This is not the story of Jack and the Beanstalk, it's more like the Deep Space movies "Don't Look Up", "Armageddon" and "Deep Impact."

And these legs go all the way down to my space boots, like Nancy Sinatra, daughter of the Chairman of the Board, says in a song,

"These boots were made for walkin and that's just what they'll do one of these days these boots are gonna walk all over you."

The pot screams at the potter, I want to be a plate or a cup, thinking if I had the power to tell the potter what I want, I would say I want to take over the power of Creation, like a squatter.

I want to swim in water like an otter, but I can't because the potter made the otter, and the female otter too, and made an animal that needs no mate, to re-create, more like procreate and you can't put a price on that Duckbill Platypus' back.

The Creator didn't give mankind sway, to attack by spaceship, or missile, or evil thought, since every word that proceeds out of the mouth was made by Him, even this thought to come an end.

Space Balls is a funny movie. Astronauts are not laughing about the question of their intimacy; it's believed hard to conceive, but who's to say what kind of Space talk rubs you the right way.

The Hubbell telescope got rid of its dirty pictures, cleaned up by a good old fashion rub a dub, and now peaks into the birth of stars, black holes, giving us earthlings a rated X-treme look see.

The Universal womb with a clue, is woman.

Why does man, who has no clue, want to tell a woman what to do with mankind that she carries inside her Universe Soul body?

This is a Circus, Circus that cuts to the nerve of us, although God makes the stars, babies are made by mystery of God, and the Bible Chronicles the history. The mystery is not clear enough to a man who can't go to Venus, yet rides on an enormous rocket, through an illusion of control.

Adam begat Seth, Seth begat Enos and Enos begat Kenan and all begotten have lost control yet give thanks for the Beatitudes blessed are the merciful. "Let There Be Light." Mercy, mercy me, on the 4th day of Creation what did we see, two great lights, to rule over day, to rule over night.

He made the stars also to shine from the firmament of heaven, down to earth, to be signs, to be Seasons, Earth Wind and Fire, Now, Then and Forever, Guiding Lights, BELO HORIZONTE. It's a woman's Right to choose, it's a woman's Right to change her

Maggiedocious Wordette

Mind, her shoes, her mood and her Right to find a way to define the days and make the rules for nights over Egypt, in Space.

The glow of my life, like a great foundation, lights up every eye that looks upon me, what did my Make Up Artist see?

Esthetician, a skin beautician, to make it shine, engulfed in a beautiful ball of exotic fire, igniting desires, and setting free dreams held back, like a beach holds back the Sea.

Within each day, let love draw forth like a child at play finds joy out of a sock, made into a toy, never let your inner child go astray, patience is a virtue every day.

Mystified by grace woven into your spine, all decisions show vison, fortitude, God's favor, no slack, and no quiver in your back. From within is the peace that calms storms of our outer fears, conflicts and tears from the milky way of constellations, not found by telescopes in Space.

Black Holes swallow all knowledge, your heart is in the clear, now here your prayers don't fail to avail you light to shine through fear.

Open the door for your mystery date, our hands reaching out instantly relate, feelings know no bounds of time we can't rewind. Let us spend our time not looking behind, just released from the emergency room, for entering a relationship too soon.

Currents of emotion sweep away thoughts of fighting the tides, as tidewaters of peace calm the eye of the storm, dry every tear that forms. Cold hands hide a warm heart, fingers reach for a new start, a patient who continues to forget, that love, don't love, nobody.

The broken pieces are too small, but his love touches places where my heart was scorned, where my heart was torn and the pain reaches out to heaven, that's where broken hearts go.

How did you get here?

Cool hand Luke would understand, J D's Revenge understands the Pointer Sisters need a slow hand, and an easy touch. Peanuts, popcorn or ice cream, a ticket for one at the movie stadium, nobody is supposed to be here, just my tears, anger and a storm of fears.

The Soul Sonnet cadence of Maggiedocious Wordette's purity.

Be the bridegroom sent from heaven, whose time I consume. Be my starship, take me up to the sky on wings of love, until they burn, flying to high as Icarus, in Greek mythology learned.

A love never dies. Who has true love, has that love to hold on to. Before I let go, I must find love untrue, unrequited, returned to sender, and don't it make your brown eyes blue.

You are specially designed, eyes are blue, eyes are green, eyes are black too, some eyes are big some eyes are small. Eyes are round like a ball, round like planet earth and round like the Sun. Some eyes see love as the world being flat, sea water falling off the edge, comes back to you.

This world view has a fire breathing dragon at the bottom of the waterfall to destroy all who fall, only the facts of love, put on the whole amour of God for you and yours. Keep in mind to always know amour means love wherever you go, just because you don't see it, doesn't mean it's not so, love never dies, it multiplies.

There's something people need; it is to be loved; to be free life is a mystery theatre with no intermission to gather yourself for what's next. There is something people need, to be able to cherish the mysterious nature of life, tomorrow is scary, please God let us know, come Lord, help us to learn your words.

We need your love to guide our way. We need each other to live as one. We need each other to reunite. We need your hand on us to show the way to Jesus, over a legion working to deceive us. We got to know where people go. We got to be where people are, that be free. We got to know, begging you please, Where do these people find new beginnings?

Heaven knows we got to know. Heaven knows we got to see what it is these people see. Heaven knows we got to live, how the sanctified people live. Heaven knows we got to know what sanctified people think, being never nervous giving to you, what is our reasonable service.

Thy rod and thy staph they comfort me, they lead me to lay by still waters, get my act right.

Still waters run deep, just an old Negro saying, not to put you to sleep, as bodies keep swaying on a limb, saying they talk "Stay Woke" to turn it anti-Black, using Mind tricks designed to turn you against yourself, and anyone that looks like you.

Speaking like your name is a joke, but it ain't, "Stay Woke." It's Gas Light, no joke, shining on you like a flashlight, neon light, a spotlight on you to make you feel a certain way, saying your name means something sad, something bad, it's the opposite of something said to make you glad.

This mental Chess move is to change your Mindset, bring shade to a slang Black people made. Scandalize skin color again. To turn your mind into an instrument that plays doubt, a hater-ade tasting like three fifth sugarless Kool-ade, not the kind your Black Daddy made, "Stay Woke."

Power to the people. Power to me, save yourself first, that's the way it has got to be, to be useful in service to thee. Jacob called Israel had a daughter, Dinah moved the Holy order, not so easy to see, surface dweller you cannot be.

A one-night stand is your demand, and that just cannot be for this "Get Christy Love" is must see TV, she is Black Coffee.

Maggiedocious Wordette

You got to dig the scene in the Bible, to know what I mean, circumcise your heart first, before we cut to the chase, Genesis 34 is the story base.

Who am I, thinking I can change things, make wrong, to do me right.

I am alone now, wishing that I could be somebody.

Wishing I could crumble the world, put it back together, to do me right.

Who am I to say that my kind of do me right, is the right kind of right to do, but we would love, not hate, I am someone who cares and she who cares, shares. I dare to open my heart, I'm who.

Word etiquette is a Maggiedocious character trip around issues, Christmas Past with tissues, and feelings of I miss you, flipping a sonnet on its head, redoing the Rhythm with some Blues.

The Savante muse leads the way for Maggiedocious Wordette to be "Wordy Rapping Hood" in a "Genius of Love" Tom Tom Club display, Tina Weymouth on Bass, husband in his Band place.

Klymaxx and "The Men All Pause," "Meeting in The Ladies Room" with Fenderella Joyce Irby and Bernadette Cooper, representing a female Band. DJ Spinderella shakes out the Salt & Peppa sound and "Push It" real good, like Black Cinderella would, for a Prince to be King.

Bring em out, bring em out, better than Christian Louboutin red bottom soles, which is his way, soul sonnet rocking the planet with Soul Sonic Force "Planet Rock" like Sugarhill Records owner Sylvia Robinson "The Message" got power to the people, "It's Good to Be the Queen."

I am no Public Enemy, with a public enema, but What Kind of Power We Got? Soul Power.

P, equals poignant, precious, polished and balanced with the perfection of God, put on trial and blazed by Holy Fire, purified, with unlimited possibly.

O, equals omnipotent, observant, obedient to God, acutely aware of ongoing attacks, knowing God will have to grant D' Evil One permission, gives man born of woman, an angels' omission.

W, equals wisdom, time made wise decisions, a gift from God not to be taken lightly, washed in Holy water reborn, willingly availing myself rightly, to be used as a vessel of The Lord wisely.

E, equal excellence, this is who God is. His goodness and mercy emerge from women, the bone that produces the flesh and the existence and the extension of life.

R, equals respect, righteousness and rebirth, which is the foundation of power. My Love is refined, and renewed with daily Bread, that is the Lord's Prayer.

Power, swing low sweet chariot, come to carry me home, I am a willing vessel from which your blessings flow to the intended. Power is fearfully and wonderfully made by God, and by woman.

Maggiedocious Wordette

Woman, you may not be able to live with her, but you cannot live without her, I'm her, she is me.

The whispers of the wind, so soft, the sound of raindrops trickling through the leaves of the trees, or the limbs, when leaves leave them. Don't leave me this way, if you gotta go, go with a smile.

For my love, you would walk the burning sands of time, it won't make sense to anyone else but you, and a man has got to do, what a man has got to do. Cloud walking, and you are free to dream with me, let me set your dreams free from slavery's captivity, swim as far as you have to; your imagination is boundless, now tell me what you see.

Construct a holy tower or your vision will go sour, the opposite of sweet, turn our good ship into defeat, the kind you wake up from screaming for relief.

Oh God! You say, that will get you close, help me Jesus! For those who won't get left behind. Your Mind is engrossed in my world, grasping each moment as special, treasuring each thought, caught within the Indian dreamcatchers' design.

A world of peace, a world of understanding, a world of love, reality asleep, dreams setting in, the existence of your Soul evolving from within. My love is Oceans wide; waves crash softly where you reside, in the middle of the universal womb, there is plenty of room in the mansion not made by man's hands.

"I knew you before you were formed in the belly," is a Godly statement, easier to understand when you speak in affirmations that you are God's plan.

Moments travel fast, memories become difficult to hold onto, causing your inner-being to get soul exhausted. In no time your special world is gone, the waves of your ocean womb turn into the sound of raindrops, tears begin their race from the well of a good place, the place within.

Serenity is an entity of blessed air that fills up the space in your lungs, cries of enmity between you and the world has weight, birth, afterbirth and rebirth, reality aware.

The sky was not gray, blue or black, fog succumbed to nature's beauty; the Sun appears to be gone away, rest assured it is shining on someone else as a new day, and a kiss is still a kiss, not to be missed standing under mistletoe.

Give a gift evergreen, a sign of peace and vitality that blooms life into winters' dormant emotions, when happiness touches your lips.

Jack and Jill went up the hill, be still and know I AM, that I AM created the cherry tree and makes you chase the rainbow. Jack and Jill went up the hill, running around an apple tree, their hearts on fire, burning like the eternal bush that Moses did see. An apple fell, hitting Jill on her crown, but it was Jack who made her love come down, and love changes is what they found.

Maggiedocious Wordette

George Washington was President first, married to Martha was he, famous for telling no lies, chopping down a cherry tree, such a gentleman. But some Plantation men had "Hidden Figures," a memoir claims one named Venus, I don't care about your other girls, "Just Be Good to Me."

And a Shirley Temple is a virgin drink that keeps things simple, Shirley Temple-Black when married, slick like LL Cool J's hit, Pink Cookies in a Plastic Bag Getting Crushed by Buildings.

Grandma says don't give away your cookies, nobody knows what her love meant like you, if you had a Grammy like mine, Bill Withers, "Grandma's Hands" should have gotten a Grammy too. Her love chastised me to write down an escape plan, not "Who Can I Run Too" Xscape Atlanta check your skin color at the gate, the Underground Railroad is coming, and you can't be late.

Harriet Tubman and run. All aboard women and men, follow the Conductor's, don't judge a helper by color of their skin, a friend is a friend that helps you in need, when you're running for freedom, a friend is a friend indeed. Before you go, hit those knees.

The Underground Railroad led to freedom from slavery, delivering African traditions and Black American bravery to change America and the world, economically, domestically and spiritually.

Tonto is the Native American of distinction, killed almost into extinction, like the buffalo, with nowhere to roam or underground railroad to run a lifeline. Let's get away from Southern States, go to the North, Canada too, through Toronto, where Black Canadians play.

Sojourner Truth was born a slave in Rifton, New York, with the name Isabella Baumfree in 1797. Isabella, showing great bravery, ran away in 1827 with her infant daughter to a White family that lived nearby and didn't believe in slavery. In 1843 Sojourner Truth was born again and became a preacher, activist, abolitionist and defender of Civil Rights and Women's Rights, she died in Battle Creek Michigan, a free Black American woman in 1883. The Truth is marching on.

Sojourner Truth gave one of the most famous speeches in the history of America in 1851, in Akron Ohio at the Women's Rights Convention. The Women's Rights National Historic Park Service gives to us this preferred, preserved version of the speech titled, **Ain't I a Woman.**

Well, children, where there is so much racket there must be something out of kilter. I think that 'twixt the negroes of the South and the women at the North, all talking about rights, the white men will be in a fix pretty soon. But what's all this here talking about?

That man over there says that women need to be helped into carriages, and lifted over ditches, and to have the best place everywhere. Nobody ever helps me into carriages, or over mud-puddles, or gives me

any best place! And ain't I a woman? Look at me! Look at my arm! I have ploughed and planted, and gathered into barns, and no man could head me! And ain't I a woman? I could work as much and eat as much as a man - when I could get it - and bear the lash as well! And ain't I a woman? I have borne thirteen children, and seen most all sold off to slavery, and when I cried out with my mother's grief, none but Jesus heard me! And ain't I a woman?

Then they talk about this thing in the head; what's this they call it? ["Member of audience whispers, "intellect"] That's it, honey. What's that got to do with women's rights or Negroes' rights? If my cup won't hold but a pint, and yours holds a quart, wouldn't you be mean not to let me have my little half measure full?

Then that little man in black there, he says women can't have as much rights as men, Cause Christ wasn't a woman! Where did your Christ come from? Where did your Christ come from? From God and a woman! Man had nothing to do with Him.

If the first woman God ever made was strong enough to turn the world upside down all alone, these women together ought to be able to turn it back and get it right side up again! And now they is asking to do it, the men better let them.

Obliged to you for hearing me, and now old Sojourner ain't got nothing more to say. [1]

Follow the North Star, let me tell you why? Keep your head up, to fulfill dreams, hopes, wishes and desires. Center your prayers in Jesus' Name, to get through whatever the world sends at you.

Everything that glitters ain't gold, for the right price, temptation could buy your priceless soul.

Count the cost infatuation pays to play on player, Mtume's version of "I'd Rather Be With you" hot passion can rule for a day and so can steamy nights, but you got to get out of bed sometime.

Gimme some Bootsy! Ah! The Name Is Bootsy Baby! Here's Bootsy! And I'm the leading lady.

"Everybody Loves the Sunshine" Ubiquity, Roy Ayers Searching, gives us 1976 Vibrations.

"Sunshower," just a sign of the power, of loving you oh baby. Sunshine and rain together, just what Dr. Buzzards Original Savannah Band ordered for the fever.

Peel me a grape, dinner at 8 don't dare be late, you better believe her.

The North Star will lead you "Far Away" from here, in a Kindred the Family Soul plan, like the Staples Singers "If You Ready (Come Go with Me). I know a place, "I'll Take You There" where ain't nobody smiling and lying to the Races.

Let Maggiedocious take you there, where we replace Race hate, look at people as Human Race, see the problem from a bird's eye view, Passover, how 7-deadly sins divide and concur you.

"Ain't no Woman Like the One I Got," Four Tops. A man with a good woman brags a lot about the good thing he's got.

A man who finds a wife, finds a good thing, and obtains the favor of the Lord, Proverbs 18:22 "She (I Can't Resist), "I just wanna be your man baby, ow, ow, ow," Jesse Johnson's Revue.

She's cold as Minneapolis ice, Ice Cream Castles in The Summertime, Morris Day and The Time what rhyme is it? Sounds of Blackness, Gary Dennis Hines, I Believe, Hold On, Soul Sonnet Holidays. Rest in Heaven's Peace, Philando Castile, 2016, Royalty.

A Song of Solomon 5:8 I charge you, O daughters of Jerusalem, if ye find my beloved, that ye tell him, that I am faint with desire of love.

This is just in time for a spiritual mountain climb, each soul sonnet is a fourteen-page rhyme and chance, for a Maggiedocious Wordette Diva dance.

"Let Me Be Your Angel" a Stacy Lattisaw song, a "Perfect Combination" duet with Johnny Gill.

Mamma I want to sing, find me as Black Cinderella, who instead of losing a shoe, gave a clue to a man who could be a king, then she unbreaks his heart with angel wings.

A broken heart doesn't believe in tomorrow, it will beg, steal or borrow for just one more chance. But everyone should know desperation shows up like perspiration and this is not a suitor's allure, presenting this scent to a woman, will chase her away for sure.

This scent of a woman would chase away a man too, if she offered as a lovesick witches' brew, an ode to the late great Jazz Icon Miles Davis, who knew.

Eau de Toilette, lightly scented, Eau de Parfum, heavy on you, take 2 aspirin, call the love doctor first thing in the morning, your praise water checkup is due.

Heaven sent, is what you prayed for, looked for by a Couple, it's what you stayed for, and you need to believe again, you need to breathe again, sings Toni Braxton.

Tony! Toni! Tone! "It Never Rains" make it rain, the "King of Sorrow" Sade, sweet is your heart to stay, never shall you let it get hollow.

Remember she who has the gold makes the rules, remind the Prince he begged Rapunzel to let down her hair, never will you be a Queen of despair.

I am Queen of Sheba, dark and lovely, King Solomon asked God for wisdom, and he loved me. The son of King David put no woman above me, his stairway to heaven made of silver and gold was a sight to behold, so were the beautiful gates that go to his porch, this soul sonnet relates.

The original stairway to heaven, you could say, and you would be right all day, pray to our father who art in Heaven, the God of our second chance, for we walk through the valley of death, as we lay, the angel of mercy gives us stay.

Not the snow angel star, how I wonder what you are, or the angel Nebula, deep in the heavens 2700 light years away.

Here's a cookie to bake your noodle, 1- light year is over 5 trillion miles away.

A light year is the distance light travels from earth in 1- year, which is to say how far light travels in a year, puts the phrase keep your head up in a new gear, giving you something to feel, truths to revere, the truth of God to overcome fear.

Open your heart, use your space ears, do you hear what I hear, No! But by reading the Holy Bible your hearing gets clearer.

Faith is stronger than man's toying with nuclear fission, nothing more powerful than God's vision, given on earth for a better life, received from Heaven for Eternal living.

I leave you with a Song of Solomon 2:1-4 I am the rose of Sharon, and the lily of the valleys. As the lily among thorns, so is my love among the daughters. As the apple tree among the trees of the wood, so is my beloved among the sons. I sat down under his shadow with great delight, and his fruit was sweet to my taste.

Trivial pursuit, a thousand points of light, various useful information, useless until the moment reveals its light. The moment will show you ready for the celestial fight, or heaven bound flight, with good news you can use, given of The Savante Muse.

Barack, Baroque

Aloha means hello and goodbye. Hawaii is paradise, tiny bubbles, in the wine, make me happy. Make me feel fine, and Don Ho takes us deeper than the original Hawaii Five O TV show.

Hawaii was grass skirts, Gillagan's Island, sunshine, coconuts, Polynesian shows and no snow, never forget The Day of Infamy, World War II, Pearl Harbor, it's the 50th State don't you know.

Are all the women beautiful, where are the ones who look like me? All the men look strong and handsome as could be. Hula dance, shake and move your hips, hula hoop hips go loop de loop.

Who knew about the Mai Tai cocktail, a mix of pineapple, orange and Rum, or Hawaiian shirts with a distinctive tropical display, their promotion brought about causal Friday.

Hawaii is the place where without delay on arrival you receive a flower necklace called a Lei, by airplane it is 6-hours from the West Coast, or 4- to 5-day Cruise.

"Far Away From Here" Kindred the Family Soul, and sadly racism can be found everywhere on the planet, but you know the Natives got Soul, and Soul food, surf and turf, rice and barbeque.

Hawaii is part of the United States, there's little league baseball, college basketball, football and sports of all sorts, a tourist destination with Cruise ships always in port.

Pro Football's All-Star Game is not in Honolulu anymore, but the game gave the States a taste of paradise Island life, attractive day and night, especially in winter.

The phrase "book em Dano" was made popular by Hawaii Five-O, so much so, slang for police became "lookout for Five-O" a street life ditty copied by Nino Brown, a gangster character in 1991 movie called New Jack City.

Who knew the delivery would be so special, the Hawaiian punch didn't come when we wanted but it was right on time in 2009.

Obama! We ladies say! He's so fine, Beach Blanket Bingo every time.

Barack, Baroque, Barak, Barack Husein Obama went from living his best life to running the whole show, down by law, Afro-Negro with more than one drop of blood from an African.

Barack Husein Obama Sr. is his father's name, he is from Kenya and Stanley Ann Dunham from Wichita, Kansas is his mother. She is white that changed the game like day to night.

Barack, Baroque

Both Parents have gone on to Glory, God accepts them just the same, Rainbow Covenant stops the rain, the promise is not to flood the world again.

The birth certificate, a trumped-up mystery, is now a golden fact of Black History, say it loud, I'm Black and I'm proud. Barry, as his friends called him, is next of kin to lots of folk, he and his wife Michelle are no joke. They go high when the opponents show how low their ethics can go.

Michelle and Barack Obama are a power couple, over the vision of 12 years a slave, a revisionist history slap back, but there's more to the big payback than reparation stacks. We got to deal with the kickbacks that hurt like a bite from a dog named snidely whiplash.

White backlash is whipping up the concept of 2-steps forward, 3-steps back, regression over progression to a post racial hate United States. The road to post racial hate is not paved, our Country continues to berate Black people as slaves and acts like it emerged from caves.

Oh behave, Ain't Misbehaving, go back to Africa, go back to where you came from, the nation of supreme immigrants, iterate and intonate there should be slavery in The United States.

Slavery is hatred, it caused a war, a wound still soar to the touch, study American history. There you will find nothing is civil about war. America's Civil War tore its soil and soul to its core.

Maggiedocious Wordette

Frankly, Scarlet I don't give a damn, but the blood buried in the soil has honor, no matter in what State you stand, "This Land is Your Land" this land was made for you and me.

MAGGIEDOCIOUS SPEAKS IN PROSE

Don't Turn Back

Walk ahead and don't turn back.
Walk with me, let me show you my dream
We will capture reality by removing each lying scheme.

Look into the future, see my seed, my baby reaches for the stars by creed.
I hear crying, the first strain to breathe, but I am here to give you all you need.

In the future awaits some locked doors,
The key is faith in the Everlasting
Time never gets old there, keep the faith.

Clusters of memory, connect the dots,
my dreams are a string of hope,
see who tells me no again and again,
though qualified, I AM denied by the color of my skin.

At times you feel inferior to them,
wishing the skin color barrier would fall,
you feel like a contagious disease,
don't inflict yourself with hate,
for their conscience bleeds.

You are not blind, the truth you can see,
Truth is motivation, faith in God is your key,
In this journey pray to stand tall and walk with me.

Fright for a season or just one night fight through darkness until daylight,
Trembling hands shake get on your knees,
Saying Lord bless my soul please.

Maggiedocious Wordette

Blind to a future that cannot be seen, a light shines through a door of faith,
The key is found on the floor by prayer, defying logic saying there's no one there,
but faith is the substance of what cannot be seen, by faith we gain more self-esteem.

Now faith is reality, no longer a dream, newly awakened to the facts,
joy comes in the morning, don't stop, don't turn back!

Barack, Baroque

Blue versus Grey, now Red versus Blue States, is the division of skin color in its modern way, sinister in all human capacity, yet the words audacity of taupe replaces the norm sarcastically.

The Audacity of Hope, Thoughts on Reclaiming the American Dream, Barack Obama's book, inspired by a great 1964 Noble Peace Prize speech by Reverend Dr. Martin Luther King Jr, and how Oslo can you go. The audacity of taupe to taint the first Black President of America, due to the color of a suit he wore in a press conference, this mendacity caused a major controversy.

The Rebel yell, and the Union ranks swell, America's family feud ain't going well, dying is the only story to tell, the 16th President of the United States knew it well. Abraham Lincoln would have to go to the inkwell, give Black men and White, the same freedom to go to hell.

Caucasus is a mountain in the world, its people are all gas and no breaks like Dick Dastardly passing you in a curve, swerving past normality with a sense of entitlement, knowing that the Race is with me, I'm sweet Polly Purebred that gets on his nerves.

Maggiedocious Wordette

A man finds a good thing when he finds a wife, a piece of heaven in this land of strife, the first Black President's Black wife. The First Lady of The United States; abbreviation Flotus, dealt well with various levels of trifling, going high when they went low, left no doubt in her show up, she put up, way up, and it's stuck forever and a day, at the end of the story a glamorous slay.

Dirty minds kept talking about f l o t u s designs from behind, there's meat on them bones, they couldn't leave her alone. The beautiful ones always break the picture, Beyonce sang "At Last" an Etta James song, Minnesota Fats didn't sing along in anticipation, if you haven't you should read Abraham Lincoln's 1863 Emancipation Proclamation.

The late great Shirley Chisolm did take a serious swing at the Presidential thing in 1972, before we had a clue, in 1968 she became the first Black Woman elected to Congress.

Come on Son, she represented New York, Bedford Stuyvesant.

Black woman leading Black man again, by any means necessary so watch your mouth, field or house Negro, when the plantation ma'am called, you had to go and play the part of Mandingo.

Barack, Baroque

Keep hope alive, Jesse Jackson 1984, again in 1988, first Black man to put on a run for the presidential cape, even William Marshall as Blacula, the first Black Vampire, couldn't drain all the bloody hate. Talk of Watergate took the cake, ate it too, a Black man President in the White House, no is the answer, there is no debate.

Black man be stereotypical, like Toucan Sam chasing fruit loops, his favorite cereal. Got milk? The thought brought new meaning to the way things used to be, keep it comedy Black man don't get serious, 1965 and the Right to vote becomes the art of the deal, it's a joke, how does it feel.

America, you have not integrated Human Rights, politics keep a filibuster fight, showcasing outright denial and delay, no fair fight or trial, only tactics to belay.

Keep taupe alive, Rainbow Coalition fights back against the flood of wickedness in high places. *"Smiling faces tell lies, sometimes they don't tell the truth, smiling faces tell lies and I got proof"* sang the group called "The Undisputed Truth" in 1972.

That's the truth Ruth, Bader Ginsberg, Flip Wilson played a female character named Geraldine who would treat Conservatives mean. The way they lied to us to get on the Supreme Court team, nudge 1973 Roe versus Wade law out, in a rehearsed scene, now here comes the judge.

Maggiedocious Wordette

Put that on my own mama, on my hood, I look fly, I look good, you can't touch my bag, wish you could. Victoria Monet sang it, Michelle Obama understood. The Senator from the hood grows up the Chicago way, run Jesse run, run for our lives, run Reverend Jackson to keep hope alive.

Barack Obama became the 44th President, despite hatred games the Grand Old Politicians play, Impeachment sought for the color of a suit. Taupe was the color, still hatred was the root of this evil pursuit, to display a symphony called White backlash during these days, and thought to be an Art of Noise, they went low, "Hallelujah Anyway."

The Barack Era, 8-years of excellence, artistically defined as bold black strokes of Mind-altering lines, turning fantasy into time captured reality, never broke, add flavor, pronounced Baroque.

"He's So Fine" gotta be mine, like the 1963 hit song from Black girl group, The Chiffons. *He's so fine, do lang do lang do lang, wish that he was mine, do lang do lang do lang.*

The Barack Era, let it be called Black Camelot, it reminded all how 1963 ended, Wind Talkers speak of the tears of Chief Sitting Bull, falling on Wounded Knee 1890 and 1973.

Remember 63' how we lost John F. Kennedy brutally on TV for all to see, white knights at the round table, and the original American Camelot be not forgot.

Barack, Baroque

America's eternal flame burns for a "Soul on Ice" Eldridge Clever paid the price of a man sold in sin, weeping eyes reaping what was sowed into the bloody dirt that screams out!

In Genesis, Cain how are you able denigrate the slain, using the same evil game again and again.

Ebonics' and the slang game still have meaning, a full Moon still lights the getaway, knowledge illuminates the Mind, put down cigarettes, healthy coffee's do the body fine, make smoke signals Uncle Tom can't find, although true allies are color blind.

Organo is not camouflage smoke, not oil to toke, it's a healthy arabica instant coffee bean, not fugazi like oregano packaged as Mary Jane, the original bag joke, like politicians stop woke.

Stay woke and don't sleep are different slang to keep track of, like the Underground Railroad runs above ground, White flight had a different sound, it was Barack Obama White people found.

"Yes, We Can" Vote for an African American. America was afloat on hope, my country tis of the Love Boat, cope with hatred, not quite, the President of the United States is Black and White.

The Pointer Sisters love him, in 1980 they sang the hit song "He's so Shy" that I relate to CHI, Deep dish pie, and the Chi-Lites from the windy City.

In the Music video Ted Lange was not just another Black guy, he played Junior on the TV show "That's my Mama" in 1974, way before Isaac the Bartender hit the floor in the 1977 hit TV show "Love Boat".

Ancestral Moms got a kick out of the news of the first Black President, made a resident alien in the White House from 2008 until 2016. Birth pain is the serpent's gift, yet a child brings joy on a celestial plain, and the mothers say you have an old soul, scandal-less.

Scandal was the name of a hit TV show about Presidential clout and doubt, but none of it came within the shadow of truth that Barack Husein Obama was about. Kerry Washington changed the game like Obama did when he unforgettably sang Al Green's classic song "Let's Stay Together" to his Queen, and the world swooned, so it seemed.

"I, I'm so in love with you. Whatever you want to do is all right with me. "Cause you make me feel so brand new. And I want to spend my life with you."

Shonda Rimes produced the Scandal TV Show, native of Chicago, her production team is called Shondaland, and Team Obama is a winning Brand, no Black Sox, just White Sox for the man.

Play your cards right, a Boston was ran on their team, trump tight, with Spades, Aces, Kings, Queens too, controlled the Joker, made the Deuce do what it do, Ireland cousins had a pint brew.

When will they ever learn? The lake of fire burns, it's a fool's gold, now ashes inside an urn. Hypocrites go sell your soul, still Barack's Art Era will forever sell well, pray tell, and let the record be shown in Chicago's Presidential Library, there's no place like home.

Nothing comes to a dreamer but a dream, so you have been told to kill your dreams before they become proclamations. Do your affirmations, study your vision wall, now what do you see?

A negative critique seeks to defeat constructive criticism, such as Barack the Community Activist was a mistake, like Mrs. Oleary's cow put fire to Chicago as America's best Steak. An Art critic's negative take cannot appreciate mere whim as the origination of imagination rippling in places once dormant, as brainwaves of thought.

In a heavenly flow, the Spirit of God moved upon the face of the waters, like The Seven Seas within a combination of words in a run on sentence, to explain how punctuation works to bring about compound thoughts of positivity, dropping a punchline, to give you an expected end.

The Baroque Era began in Italy, it is noted for layered structure, energetic tempo and expressive movement, its influence defining poetry, architecture, art, fashion and music from 1600 to 1750.

Maggiedocious Wordette

Speaking the word Baroque helps your diction and acutes the ears to Symphony music as a prescription for peace, when hearing the violin strings of Concerto number 1, Spring in E Major, composed by Vivaldi. The Four Seasons complete are Concerto number 2, Summer in G Minor, Concerto number 3, Autumn in F Major, and Winter Concerto number 4, in F Minor. Bravo.

Maggiedocious gives a show from Symphony to Frankie Valli "Can't Take My Eyes Off You" call it Baroque too, but it's Barack when he enters a room, or leaves, it's an Era gone too soon.

The world knows the temporal renditions of Handel's Messiah and Corelli's Christmas melodies, you can believe a Symphony follows the arcs and depths of a girls' moods, influencing her to be an influence on him, passive aggressive manipulation at the end of a whim.

Maggiedocious Wordette gets it done, Black Girls Run, Deanie the Yogini, Black Girls Brunch, Black Girl Vice President, Senator Kamala Harris packs a punch. Money? She'll take your lunch.

Do the girls run this mutha?

"We Are the World" curtsey, wave your wrist then twirl, R.E.S.P.E.C.T Aretha Franklin forever. The Queen of Soul is good as it gets, Beyonce asked the question with music, the answer is yes.

Barack, Baroque

Baroque adds color to the one, two, step, added the harpsicord to instrumentation and complex vocal arrangements to sound. Casting wit and style like Texas Representative Jasmine Crocket's recipe for dissidence, which is go from head to toe in acerbic assertation of a woman's attempt to discomfit you, then call out a bad built butch body with logic, passed on by Grandma's hands.

Ciara, featuring Missy had a hit song in 2004 titled 1, 2 Step, they can tell you all about the Barack Era Whitehouse concerts, which put R&B and fashion together, Gala like the MET.

A chorus from The Jones Girls song "*I Just Love the Man*" features the blood sisters talking and singing about real problems on the 1980 album titled, At Peace with Woman.

"I just love the man, I don't care what you say I just love the man `Cause he treats me the way that I want to be treated, when I need to be needed when it comes to lovin me he's alright."

And when a man loves a woman can't keep his mind on nothing else, he'll trade the world for the good thing he's found, Percy Sledge sang this powerful song in 1966, it was a number 1 hit everywhere people heard it, I think because straight to the heart it hits.

Love has no black or white skin tones, and it does take a fool to learn love don't love nobody, love makes the world go around, like the original Detroit Spinners did. Don't burn rubber on me, you got a fast car, a mighty love will drive you far. I've learned to respect the power of love sang Stepanie Mills, who led the 1975 WIZ Broadway production singing, when I think of "Home".

Look back at this lyrical road to find lines from Tracy Chapman, Deon Jackson, The GAP Band and The Spinners. Jesus is love sings the Commodores, listen, and it will open your heart doors.

"Jesus loves me this I know for the Bible tells me so. Little ones to Him belong; they are weak, but He is strong.
Yes, Jesus loves me! Yes, Jesus loves me!
Yes, Jesus loves me! The Bible tells me so."

Anna Bartlet Warner wrote Jesus loves me as a poem in 1859. In 1861 William B. Bradford pinned the music tagalong, 7.7.7.7.7. count with refrain, Soul Sonnets, sometimes do the same.

Barack, Baroque, Barak, pronounced bey-rock, a military leader in the book of JUDGES, with Prophetess Deborah, Judge of Israel. Barak prayed the Prophetess tagalong in battle, not as a cookie, but a girl scout of prayer power, that brings on God's victory in a sanctity shower.

Barack, Baroque

A married woman can lead a Nation through War and Peace, with no one asking about her competency, we hold these truths to be self-evident. A woman can be President of the U.S.A. working with men whose parliamentary act leaves them standing on the verge of getting it on.

Barack, Baroque, Barak, no it's not West Indian Patois, a rhythm slang that has a Geechee twang, it's an island thing, murder she wrote means a whole different thing. Boss Lady running the show only you can touch my body. I get that from my mama, black don't crack, I look fly, I look good.

Barack, Baroque, Barak, Earth, the 3rd rock from the sun. Michelle Obama is a beautiful one that didn't break the picture, babe this Black woman in the Oval Office turned a prince into a king.

We're not done, gimme Sommore, it's not funny but a comedian can make you laff, yes, she can.

Can you hear Barack Obama in 2008 saying, **don't tell me we can't change. Yes, we can. Yes, we can change. Yes, we can. Yes, we can heal this nation. Yes, we can seize our future.**

Yes, We Can, Chicago house music lent Barack a hand, Baroque in its Art, Barak in its fighting plan. Got to talk about the O before we're done, that one hit the Gräfenberg scale, Barak got help from a woman named Jael, she pinned downed the enemy with a nail.

Maggiedocious Wordette

Oprah built Harpo studio in Chicagoland and gave the original Barack a stage on which to stand, Ophrah in the book of Judges too, is a land made holy for an angel to come through, it's a divine allegorical coincidence for you. She's quite funky, funky as you can get, 1980 female Funkadelic group Parlet, singing "Wonderful One" on the album "Play Me or Trade Me" it's hard to get.

The Butterfly effect is your daily flight through life, the vanity of your beauty gives way to your spiritual duty to honor the flowers in the Lord's Garden with prayer power, given to you by the lily in the valley.

This is the desired effect, sufficient in its subtleties, you sip ripples of reality, girl power keeps you on top, your eyes on the prize seen through Barack, Baroque, Barak.

MAGGIEDOCIOUS SPEAKS IN PROSE

Silhouette

The strength of a Black man cannot be defined by an outer frame.

His strength comes from within, though his silhouette exudes power.

A deliberate creation from ancestral foundations to stand strong with a desire to strive for upper echelons and dominions since conception.

Black man come out, do not hide, you fight with a lion's pride and standalone having to prove you are a whole man, years before you are grown.

I don't want to be alone tonight, I am your light, follow my path, know that it is right. In this world you struggle, living takes a toll, makes boys to men, fast a child's life unfolds, you cry beneath the soul, emotion forbidden to see, falls into past tense when you're with me.

Black to the future is my declaration to your core, you've got inner strength, I'll give you more. Though your silhouette exudes power, failure is the prevailing view, then discernment of reality through all the world throws at you, God imparts the ability to think, renewed strength.

Could it be a thoughts' conception is formed by the breath of God, who did move the waters of the world, in the beginning. God's Breath, the silhouette transforming a universal void into the firmament of heaven, filled by stars, planets and earth's life sustaining creation.

Maggiedocious Wordette

Black man, take hold of love from heavens' length above, stand a nation on solid foundation, take my hand that God imparts, as a helpmeet for your heart.

Clarity reigns, strength rises above all weakness, this is the power of a man's reality transformed, no one can touch what the spirit builds. Two become one, woman conceives the seeds that breed the next division of life's mystery. A strength renewed, an ancestral challenge met by open arms, lay your head upon my breast, in me whole man, it is okay to rest your beautiful silhouette.

MAGGIEDOCIOUS SPEAKS IN PROSE
The Vote

There came a point in my life when an important election was pending, time to cast the vote, arc of the moral universe bending.

Two opponents want the vote, it's time to make a choice, they try to influence me with all they have and their voice.

I sit in contemplation, their voices are slick and quick but how did one know my wish list, promising me everything he will get, everything he will do, it sounded too good to be true.

Confusion torments me, I become unsure, then I get a feeling the vote will be the cure. I was afraid of my choices, seeing by faith is blind sight, hearing the slick voice confused me, something just ain't right.

I felt like giving up this task, but voting is important to do the opponents sound similar, only one voice speaks the truth. Scratch a lie to catch a thief, and yes that is the whole truth, for within his speech you will find the one who's not 100 proof.

Promises piqued my curiosity, I was shown a grandiose time,

Promised again there would be no struggles, no worries,

The slick voice says the world would be mine.

I was puzzled, my heart burned, this is not a good fit,

Yearning, learning my mind returns to say,

Maggiedocious Wordette

Lofty promises did not earn my vote on this election day.

Black woman, fight for the Rights of a world created through you,

In a chain of fools, don't lie to yourself, that's a Golden rule. We, Shall, Over, Come, **Cast The Vote**, It Is Done.

MAGGIEDOCIOUS SPEAKS IN PROSE
No Ballot Needed

Woman, Black woman searching
Your wish is my command
I will treat you better, than he can,
put the finer things of life in your hands.

Sincerity whispers in my ear, agape love.

Woman, Black woman
Make peace and love a reality,
Defeat fear and anxiety and together
We will help society, shine great as the Sun.

An important election is pending
The pressure to cast my ballot was non ending.

There are only two opponents in this race
The stakes are too high to make a mistake.

They both want to win, the goal is my soul,
Eat, drink, laugh, we're all born into sin.

Good, better, best, bad, try them, to influence my soul.
Your needs will be met, treat everybody right, sounds better than steal, cheat, take by might.

My heart knows the voice from above, always a step ahead, always giving thoughts of Eternity and Salvation instead of dread. Woman, Black woman, some have begged and some have pleaded, but for you walk into Heaven, **No Ballot Needed.**

Maggiedocious Wordette

MAGGIEDOCIOUS SPEAKS IN PROSE
I Pray

Each day I awake
I thank you Lord
for this day
And many more.

If you will
take my hand
help me to understand
Your word and your plan.

Give me wisdom
where ignorance falls,
let me know love
when hate is involved.

The road I travel
if it is wrong,
guide my feet
make me strong.

Where there is darkness
show me the light,
through the turbulence
strengthen my fight.

Your Will I shall do
No matter how difficult
a task remains; I shall endure
through ridicule or pain.

Each day LORD! I succeed
by Your strength; I know
You will never let me go.
 In Jesus' Name I Pray
Amen.

Maggiedocious Wordette

My First Christmas Away From Home

You're a big girl now, no more daddy's little girl, pig tails are grown up, your curls have Bangs and you make your own bucks. Dunkin' makes my coffee when I'm away but never far did I roam, until that day I will forever remember, my first Christmas away from home.

I am a Stylistics, modern in all things, computer proficient and when I'm not teaching, I learn. Home is where the heart is, wherever Mamma lays her hat, she makes a nest, good, better, best.

I love my parents' home, they taught and encouraged me, saying you'll do well on your own, but not even their loving words, prepared me for my first Christmas away from home.

Christmas is my favorite time of the year, every time it comes around it finds me in good cheer. I'm the one who hangs all the mistletoe, it's me who gets the first kiss, it's me that Santa didn't miss, and I make angels in the snow.

I build the best snowmen, playful snowball fights a plan, a brothers' love, a sisters' too, I always make a task, for each of us to do.

Hello Christmas, once again, we greet each other like loving friends, back together again, I know your secret, know you're misunderstood, understand your power, commercialized and considered the opposite of good.

My First Christmas Away From Home

I saw mommy kissing Santa Claus, and I sing the Temptation's version of "Silent Night," in my Mind, baby it's could outside, and it's me who keeps the fireplace burning with delight.

I kept watch of the clock, my plans were good, but this spoiled girl would have to take no this Christmas time, and this rhyme is not making sense to my heart.

I would if I could come home for Christmas Day, I promised my Christmas friend that I would never miss this holiday, but unforeseen circumstances will keep me away.

The Joke goes, hey do you want to make God laugh? Well tell him what your plans are!

Stay Woke! Stop Woke is a joke, listen with a black ear, then you can you hear God laughing.

Caring is a word few understand, rare like the smoothness of a rose petal, created by the touch of God's Hand. Caring is a quality that cannot be artificially generated from an artificial start, it is a reflexive emotion from a good heart, a strong will manifests the love it imparts.

I care about the incidents of coincidence revolving around the innocence of random acts of love and kindness, properly received as godly recompense. A positive over negative reaction like the birth of Christmas represents.

Suddenly life has new meaning to me, I'm a Caribbean Queen with a Billy Ocean of knowledge to battle responses to the question, "How old is Christmas?"

Maggiedocious Wordette

Christmas means great things to me, although I don't remember my first picture on Santa's knee, the date says I was three. I remember 1st grade, a picture with Santa Claus and I thought I had it made. I asked Santa for a new bike with training wheels, so I could learn to ride fast, like I did on my Big Wheel.

The in-store Santa always wanted to know how old I was, and the truth I always told, believing in the miracle of Christmas, never are you too old. How old is too old before for the truth of Santa is told? Different strokes for different folks, is what I am told.

She'll be riding 6 white horses when she comes, but I was clueless in the saddle, sleepless too, I felt like little Cindy in Whoville not knowing what to do. I'll go to a doctor, Doctor Suess will do, the Grinch stole Christmas, but he gave it back too.

Space the final frontier, to boldly go to Christmas Past or Future, without Present day fear holding back the years, "Simply Red" Simply put, never mix ole Saint Nickolas with the bible Old Testament that stands in time before Christmas, when years step back Daniel San! Like the Next Karate Kid, what a girl wants, that's the movie Hillery Swank did.

Before Christ, BC, means step back the years, show the naked truth all the way to ground zero, yes to the backless dress and zero is my hero. Christmas means the years now go forward from ground zero, no longer do you subtract, BC ends, AD 1 begins, baby Jesus is our hero.

The New Testament starts the years again, because Christmas is the new beginning my friend, never mistake Jesus Christ and Santa Claus again.

My First Christmas Away From Home

Christmas means to me, lift every voice and sing, keep hope alive and the angels sing hallelujah! Christmas means God Bless us, everyone, with toys for tots, and big toys for big girls and boys. Christmas means somewhere on the dinner table will be collard greens, sweet potato pie and who likes mince pie, Rufus and Chaka Khan, who will *stop on by*.

Where is the Grinch, I'm sure it was he who pinched every little inch of time I was to have spent, looking out into the field from my favorite bay window bench. The thought never crossed my Mind that this would be the very first time I missed Christmas at home, I thought I was in control, no one can tell me what to do, I'm on my own. I paid the cost to be the boss, I make lemons into lemonade and always carry the hot sauce, rain, sleet or snow I'll be ready to go, but a funny thing happened to me on the way to Christmas Day, not by planes, trains or automobiles could I make my way home.

This time I would have to stay in my place, my home away from home, where my heart would have to be, everything that could go wrong did go wrong, against me.

Who can translate my words to heaven? Who comforts but the Comforter. To whom do you pray? Don't be blind, the help that comes from the hills, is the Holy Spirit left behind.

Anyone can be rehabbed, perhaps inspired by sinner turned saint name Rahab, looking to the hills from whence comes my help, Exodus 16:9-10

Snowflakes of love falling on me, I picture vividly, walking hand and hand with my puppy love, dreaming about what gifts would be for me, under the Christmas tree.

Maggiedocious Wordette

Will he get a gift for me, a mistletoe kiss innocently? Snowflakes and Christmas go hand and hand but "Christmas in Jamaica" sings Tony Braxton, bringing sensuous to the big girl party, singing "Santa Please" and "Pretty Please."

You know the way Tony breathes, making you forget about a cold weather Christmas, with her "Snowflakes of Love" CD, listening on an island sand trap that hits where the sun don't shine, hot temperatures, cold wine, a Holiday of a different kind.

How many ways do I love you? Let me count the ways, there's one for every day the Earth goes all the way around the sun. "Christmas time is here" sung by Tony Braxton makes it clear.

I just don't want to be lonely this year, but I'll be alone, it's my first Christmas away from home.

No need to make a "Home Alone" 4 movie, alone for Christmas is not what I want to see, but my schedule says that's the way it will have to be.

Do you love Christmas?

Not being home for the Holiday Season is an emotional tragedy without reason.

Put the Magic of The Blue, Christmas album on a record player, and a magic sideshow will be my getaway on vinyl.

I can hardly wait for Christmas, January's slow, February snow, Spring it takes so long, Summer's hardly gone, and I can't wait, sings The O' Jay's.

Birds of a feather flock together, fly south for the warm weather, give a dog a bone click your heels 3 times, because there's no place like home.

My First Christmas Away From Home

MAGGIEDOCIOUS Speaks In Prose

Christmas Everlasting Friend

My Fondness of you is hard to describe
I think about you with a twinkle in my eye.
We share life in different ways, we laugh,
we talk with providence, we pray.

My Christmas Everlasting friend
I look upon you discretely,
Watching your perplexing ways,
I've come to understand them more each day.

The concepts you form, carried out with strength,
show me how to persevere and be strong in a storm.

My Christmas Everlasting friend
you accept what is right,
cast out what is wrong
re-evaluating the complex,
knowing where you belong.

You are my best friend for life, a sparkling Gem,
there when I needed you, on you I can depend.
You listened with sincerity and with frankness you spoke,
ascertaining my dignity, helping me to cope.

The love I see in you keeps my head held high,
as to follow the North Star in the sky.

The star is to the night,
as the leaf is to the tree,
the star light is you, the star light is me,
Christmas Everlasting friend.

Maggiedocious Wordette

I always make it back home at Christmas, distant miles, travel time, add more charms on my bracelet, I work hard for the money, what I want I get. Failure is not an option, it's a game show I don't play, what's My Line? I'm hustling every day.

I'm the Bag lady now. I have gift bags for everyone, I'll send them alone or they go without me. I need a cup of tea, make me feel fine, can't let commercialism get the best of me, Kwanzaa time Erykah Baduizm in a "Window Seat" the day after Christmas, African Americans Umoja meet.

One by one they come, preoccupied with activities of the day, talking on cell phones, walk on by, making it easy to hide sorrowful tears dropping from my eyes. Who is the female pied piper, Maggie go lucky, yes, then I return to my regular program.

I think God, as an angel unaware, gently interrupted me as a stranger, who with a polite gesture, communicated by sign language, saying hi! Just like that sadness said goodbye, "Walk on by" like Dionne Warwick sings, but I will be joyful on purpose Christmasing.

Sunshine, lollipops and rainbows. Everything that's wonderful is what I feel when we're together. Brighter than a lucky penny, when you're near the rain goes, disappears, dear, and I feel so fine just to know that you are mine

In 1963 Lesley Gore sang that and more, it's my party and I can cry if I want to.

My First Christmas Away From Home

The Christmas blue magic sideshow will not be a 3-ring circus of tears, messing up my makeup, because me and my Holiday plans break up.

Who knew Christmas could give me the blues, tell me Mommy what am I to do? Has this ever happened to you, and if it did, how did you get through?

Tell me Daddy what about you, do you remember your first Christmas away from home, can you give me a clue? Please help me find a way to get through. Tell me Brother, tell me Sister, what am I to do? Does the Ghost of Christmas Past come to help Christmas Present be good to you.

Mamma said, Daddy said, Brother and Sister spoke the same words, pray and pray some more, that's what you do. Keep on praying, giving thanks, when the answers come to you.

I thank you Lord for many things, just to sit down by your side, gives true meaning to the words ride or die. I thank you Lord for what each day brings, may it be bad, good, rough, or smooth, I know that you will forever rule.

I know Lord that it is you who creates the air I breathe, that it's you who taught my lungs to receive. I know Lord, it's you who makes the heart pump blood constantly, with pressure to keep the flow, never too high, staying alive, never too low, and it's you Lord who restores my soul.

O Lord! When I forget to tell you, please always know, it's me, it's me O Lord! Who loves you so

Maggiedocious Wordette

Life is like a seed; planted in our mother's womb, growing slowly, always protected but soon we must leave the room, take a leap of faith, open to life as rose petals, patiently running the race.

Let the Mind conceive that we are born of a seed, with a seed of love inside, evil is a learned reflex, when the spirit of love is denied. Love is fruit from heaven, where our Lord God resides.

God, who knew you before you were formed, Christ thy Savior is born, no more room at the Inn, though you will be told contrary, earth is temporary, the Bible is where this information is buried.

When we are in full bloom our flower adds to life, a rose showing its beauty has a purpose to collect its nectar and pass it on in a butterfly effect.

The butterfly's flight here to there overcomes negativity, connecting our lives one to one with the positivity of the love nectar it injects, the effect from original wave virgin Mother Mary projects.

Jesus is not the Elf on a shelf, Santa Claus or anybody else. It's easy to begin feeling blue when you make Christmas all about you. I'll be so blue, Christmas without you, but shake a hand, give of yourself, to help someone else off the selfishness shelf.

It's better to give than to receive, Jesus is the reason for the Season, be a helper and lend a hand if you can believe. Meek and humble, always maintaining, we ascertain the beauty of the rose, learning how to close

My First Christmas Away From Home

our petals, to open them again as a testimony to show our metal.

My first Christmas away from home is not a sign that I have been rejected, it is love reflecting that I am blessed, to be a blessing. Let this be a lesson to open my heart, for someone will be in my path whose new life will start from prayers God respected.

Again, looking to the hills from whence comes my help, I catch subtleties designed to appease my anxieties, warm like a summer breeze teasing my nose. But in winter, the cold tickles my toes, each hint constructed within impossible coincidence, inducing meditation that springs into reflection and introspection, producing a Butterfly Effect.

The Butterfly Effect is what you get when emotions and memories connect Christmas Past with Christmas Present, stuck in time without a Christmas Future. I remember the first time I made a wish for a gift, then found it under the Christmas tree, I knew Mommy and Daddy had gotten it for me and they said thanks be to God, who knows all your wishes.

Like He arose from the dead, let us return to that warmth of the womb, the universal cocoon, the star child birthing room, a Nebulae waiting.

A Nebulae waiting is a soul sonnet stating all Stars form in huge clouds of gas and dust, thus is the mysterious touch of the Creator of all things. Yet there is this thought, it may be a small thing to a few, my first Christmas away from home is a kick in the caboose.

"A star stood still on yonder hill, praise God that star still shining still. And we shall share in the glory of love because a star stood still, that night a star stood still."

Lyrics from a Christmas song titled "A Star Stood Still (Song of The Nativity)" written by Barbara Ruth and Johnny Broderick, sung by Mahalia Jackson on her 1962 Silent Night Album.

It came upon the midnight clear, that glorious song of old, from angels bending near the earth to touch their harps of gold; "Peace on earth good will to men, from heaven's all-gracious King."

These lines open the 1849 poem "It Came upon The Midnight Clear" written by Edmound Sears then made into a Christmas Carol, greatly sung on the 1968 "Christmas with Mahalia" album.

Hear and feel the words it takes to create a soul sonnet, seek multiple connections when you look within this spoken word book. Spoken word performance in written format, built to entertain your spiritual third eye, answering questions you didn't ask, attaching new tasks at a whim, skimming the waves, it's a woman's prerogative to control, or want to be saved, rich never wretched, we are the butterfly effect that got men to leave the caves.

My First Christmas Away From Home

"Diamond to the pearls of love, If I could, I would give you the world. But all I can do is just offer you my love, if I gave you diamonds and pearls, would you be a happy boy or a girl,"

Lyrics by Prince and the New Power Generation and then there is Marilyn Monroe in another diamond of a sing along song "Diamonds Are a Girls Best Friend."

"Men grow cold as girls grow old and we all lose our charms in the end but square-cut or peal-shaped these rocks don't lose their shape Diamonds are a girl's best friend."

Woman is the first gift a man could get, there's nothing that's come along to top us yet, but Jewelry is tops on a girls Christmas list.

Prince Rogers Nelson in another music iteration, formed a girl band named "3rdEyedGirl" **Another love** is the first song they sing.

"You said I was what you wanted Liar, liar, you never wanted me that way I was just something you flaunted hired and fired You never had a plan to stay if you don't like it 'round here Find another love,"

With your third Eye opened, there's something easy to see, unearthed within carefully crafted soul sonnet obscurities, drawn to the light, there is no trap and no got cha, in my butterfly effect. I'm not crying, you're crying, you would cry too, the first time this happened to you, tears for fears, and everybody wants to rule the world.

Maggiedocious Wordette

In God we trust, perception and understanding are realities, mercifully given in small sips, lips that launched universal dreams, pleasures, sights to behold and treasure, wise men will keep hold.

My First Christmas Away From Home

MAGGIEDOCIOUS Speaks In Prose
A Merry Christmas with Love

It Took a Year to Get Here

Our Gift From Above.

REJOICE!

A Blessed Season for Us

Celebrating the Birth of Christ Jesus.

God Gave His Only Son

His Kindness,

His Wisdom,

His Special Love.

A Promise Never Ending

A Love Everlasting,

A Spirit on Whom We Can Depend.

Reflect On This Joyous Day

Search From Within,

Radiate the Feeling

Our New Life Begins,

A Merry Christmas with Love.

Maggiedocious Wordette

I'll be home for Christmas, you can count on me, please have snow and mistletoe and presents under the tree. Christmas Eve will find me where the love light gleams, I'll be home for Christmas, if only in my dreams.

These lyrics are part of the song "I'll Be Home for Christmas" written in 1943 by Kim Gannon and Walter Kent, made famous by Harry Lillis "Bing" Crosby Jr. Bing, the old crooner, also sung "White Christmas" written in 1942 by Irvin Berlin, both noted as most popular Christmas songs.

In my family home those songs were popular, and stand alone, but they don't contend with the Black Christmas Anthem "This Christmas" (Hang All the Mistletoe) by Donny Hathaway, 1970 or "Chestnuts Roasting on an Open Fire" by Nat King Cole released in 1960.

Black Butterfly effect for Christmas was always respect for Jesus, Joseph and Mother Mary, it is the greatest story ever told. Never forget the magic of the Season as it unfolds, and just like the wind blows, you will not know from where the spirit comes, but you know when it goes.

Christmas comes but once a year, I will pray we can be together next year, and my prayer will never stop, Jesus is love, this is what we got. Christmas lingers 12 days strong, New Year Eve and New Year Day have had their way, the Holiday ain't over until Epiphany, January 6th, known around the world as 3-Kings Day.

My First Christmas Away From Home

Dressed to kill, in beautiful lingerie, alone I lounge on the day before Christmas, black butterfly, take me away let me retrace your flight. I want to see what you pick up, and how you displace the grace of the Season, I'm determined not to waste.

A Butterfly's flight path has no simple logic flower to flower, the effect radiates sweet and sour. The effect flows backwards, sideways, stirs the drink, leads, follows and builds a think tank, existing no matter what men think of a concrete rose, within soul sonnets and prose.

My kingdom for a kiss, behold, that man would sell his soul. Sow the seed of wisdom into every cloud we reign, once man looked at woman, the world has not been the same.

Let the dead bury their own dead but you go ahead, tell it on the mountain high, the valley low, tell it everywhere you go. Christmas Present is not a commercial we make to pretend, it is a gift given in the year before time ends, when 1 BC counts down to zero, making baby Jesus our hero.

Christ was not born in BC, Before Christ, Jesus Christ was born, then AD years start from Zero.

BC to AD is not a band, although you do have the ADC Band, which hit the R&B chart in 1978 with their song "Long Stroke" a memory lost in smoke obscurity to you, unless you P-Funk.

ADC Band was the plan of a Black woman, Kaiya Matthews and a Black man, Michael Judkins.

Put a long stroke at the end of BC - and begin – AD, then brush up on your Spanish with me, on we go to the Three Degrees - Love Message when we translate anno domini.

AD stands for *anno domini, which translated means,* **in the year of our Lord.** Love is the message that I bring to you if you thought AD meant after-death.

We three kings have traveled far, following the shining bright North Star, the Epiphany we bring 12 days after the Angels sing, Christ thy Savior is born.

Gold, Frankincense and Myrrh, a gift from each king, on which we can concur.

In 1857 American Clergyman John Henry Hopkins Jr wrote "We Three Kings of Orient are" while living in Vermont, it is a great Christmas Carol for singing.

From around the world this soul sonnet brings facts and interesting things to the Spirit of the Holiday, forever Evergreen.

A beautiful picture on butterfly wings, the breath of romance her flight does bring, hang all the mistletoe the world sings.

Memories will do, to make room for a brand – new Christmas present.

I'll have to channel my inner Eartha Kitt, re-enact her unforgettable 1953 hit song "Santa Baby" about what's on her Christmas wish list, singing of gifts she wants to get.

My First Christmas Away From Home

"Santa baby, a '54 convertible too, light blue, I'll wait up for you, dear Santa baby, so hurry down the chimney tonight. Think of all the fun I've missed, think of all the fella's, that I haven't kissed. Next year, I could be just as good, if you check off my list. Santa baby, I want a yacht, and really that's not a lot, Been an angel all year, Santa baby, so hurry down the chimney tonight."

It's my first Christmas that I stand alone.

I prepared all year to celebrate with friends and family at the family home, where sweet memories are mine to own. My own place is where I must stay, my hometown is too far away.

What do the lonely do at Christmas?

I don't know and I won't know, soon my home away from home will be a Holiday sight to see, when I put up my own Christmas tree, I'll start right now so Christmas Day won't miss me.

Go with me to November 1971, the Christmas Season for boys and for girls growing out of their teens, soon to be young ladies know what "The Stylistics" sing, "You're A Big Girl Now."

"You can love, girl, if you must, you can kiss, girl, if you must, what you'll see day by day all the realness in your way, and you're a big girl now, no more daddy's little girl."

You can perceive the mercy and grace of your daily flight through life, to be a black butterfly is Cause and

Maggiedocious Wordette

Effect, ripples of time multiply realities we all will sip, let us stay humble with the power a girl gets. God's highest server, fly's low on earth, and waves of subtleties the seeds get.

Christmas is in the Heart, that I will never forget.

My First Christmas Away From Home

MAGGIEDOCIOUS Speaks In Prose

<u>A Sweet, Sweet Blessing</u>

Today the Sun rises, a clear, beautiful day,
its rays smiling through, sweet blessings coming your way.

The warmth brings reminders, of days gone by,
some filled with laughter, with others wanting to cry.

The Sun rises, each day anew, happy or sad,
God gave you sweet blessings, all that He had.

What beauty God created, a strong woman indeed,
standing steadfast in what you believe.

Your love unending, your words powerful
Your life an example for the generations of tomorrow.

Merry Christmases are in the air, and as sure as the jolly wind blows,
God gave sweet blessings for every man, woman and child to share.

The world has been blessed, I'm a witness.
A special day is now in the past, but oh! how I wished it would last.

Today the Sun sets, a clear, beautiful day
A precious memory stays deep in thy heart.
A sweet blessing, you have been,
A Sweet, Sweet Blessing that never ends.

Maggiedocious Wordette

The End.

Maggiedocious Wordette's Soul Sonnets

Companion book is Soul Sonnet's Part II, The Sadie Hawkins Revue.

Epilogue

I have always loved rhymes and was proud of myself when I began to connect thoughts in a cadence, like a drill sergeant in the movies. I love limericks, which are 5-line poems that end with a surprise punchline, made popular in Ireland. I have an affinity for fairytales and that's how Maggiedocious Wordette comes to life in my adult Christian fiction story, from Ghost of Christmas Past to a woman who speaks poetically about everyday matters.

Sonnets were developed in Italy; they must follow a certain pattern of sound with rhymes that end in 14-lines. It is from this premise I imagined Maggiedoucious Wordette to be a Soulful Sonnet, unconfined, waxing poetic with a rhythm and blues subset 14 pages long.

The Christmas Connoisseur is a title I've obtained from my Niece Nakia Dewberry, who wrote the Foreword for my first book, and it is the title of the first chapter of this book. Maggiedocious is from the Mary Poppins movie song Supercalifragilisticexpialidocious, which means extraordinarily good, and that's what this character represents to me.

It is wonderful to see the new beginning that every Christmas is, and I put that feeling into Soul Sonnet Holidays. The new beginning is this first of a kind new book, it is a gift which springboards me into continuing the characters from Hang All The Mistletoe as a franchise.

Chapter 4, Barack, Baroque featured the poem titled **The Vote**, it will forever be a reminder of the troubles in American politics and our Yes, We Can, hope and our Yes, she can spirit that will prevail, as it always has. Prayer Changes things.

I love to write. Becoming a published Author was a big accomplishment, putting this story together was fun and challenging. It was by faith that I continued this line of storytelling, prayers helped me when I got lost representing a female character through 14 pages of rhymes. God Bless you for reaching this point, think of it as 42 Generations, chromosomes and me, John Gary Dewberry, presenting Maggiedocious Wordette, to you and to the world. I want this book to be a Holiday for your Soul. Let Peace be a Blessing!

Afterword

I had fun authoring this book, it gave me an opportunity to be creative with poetry, music and rhyming in a way that is fresh and new to book readers. I wanted to do it as a challenge to my writing, since there was nothing like Soul Sonnets on the market. Soul Sonnet's gave me the ability to take the concept and be creative, moving thoughts of Christmas into other subjects.

Maggiedocious Wordette is the Prophetic Spirit that enters your life to bring back the joy of Christmas by showing you the good, bad and ugly sides of what it was, and how it is.

This Spoken Word book; as a story concept, was a leap of faith to feature her character from Hang All the Mistletoe, Meet the Black Ebenezer Scrooge; my first book, where she met the world as the Ghost of Christmas Past. This plot reminded me of the female ghost in the classic retelling of Charles Dickens, A Christmas Carol movie titled Scrooged, though she played The Ghost of Christmas Present, I like it and hope to expand my character to stage and television.

Maggiedocious is my wife, Karen S. Ware Dewberry. In my research to put a second book on the market, I read her poems, thoughts and musings written from 1987 - 2005, which she kept in a 3-ring binder, then asked if I could use them for a book. She, being humble, said use them if you like them, but I was just writing stuff down to help me get through some things.

I was enthralled with her work; it forced me to see from a woman's point of view. I knew of the personal nature she wrote about, and her expressions moved me. I developed the woman ghost of Christmas Past to be in my original story, the revelation came to me for a Black Woman to be her and speak in a poetic flow, which has brought me a new respect for writers of poetry.

Thank you for reading my spoken word book, in which itself is an impossibility made reality in the sense that a spoken word is not written down. But the thought is not only written down, it was also turned into Soul Sonnets, that live through a character birthed of man and wife, raised to be a present help in this world of need, indeed, Maggiedocious Wordette is all of that.

There is more instore for readers to explore, Maggiedocious Wordette is real, she is more than a figment of my imagination. I give thanks to a myriad of spiritual circumstances from which my vision of this woman has emerged from the Underground railroad, to go to the Moon and beyond, and from NO WHERE TO NOW HERE. Can you dig it sugar? Cool Beans.

Biography

Author, John Gary Dewberry

This adventure into writing is not new for the Author, there are business proposals and creative entertainment projects on the shelf and within file cabinets. Soul Sonnets is a culmination of these experiences and an extension of his first book titled Hang All the Mistletoe, Meet the Black Ebenezer (HATM)

John felt the Christmas tradition of newfound joy on Christmas morning needed an uplifting Black family perspective, conveyed through storytelling like Charles Dickens a Christmas Carol, written in 1843, affected rich and poor people. Christian Fiction gets full treatment with the development of Maggiedocious Wordette, as the Ghost of Christmas Past, into a standalone book. The city of North Star Village and the characters created in HATM now have a launch pad to focus Christmas on the reason for the season, which is Jesus Christ.

John was ordained as Pastor in April 2023, shortly after HATM was published, and will always relate to the way the great spiritual giant Reverend Dr. Martin Luther King Jr. formed godly chants to water the seeds of word craftsmanship and storytelling. Dr. King is the substantial influence on inclusion in all things that are American life that gives John, as a Black Author, the imagination and confidence to produce a story for books and movies that place Black people as the main subjects, not a side story.

Anyone reading this Biography, who read Soul Sonnets, will understand John's Hometown Springfield Massachusetts connection to rhymes, through Dr. Seuss, (whose name is Theodore Geisel, known as Dr. Seuss, 1904 – 1991). A Dr. Seuss book fed curiosities and encouraged the mind to research and write down thoughts, as his words encouraged children and adults to enjoy reading.

Reading is fundamental to John and there is an enjoyment you can sense, that flows though the subjects and story to story. You can tell that John came up during the great times of the Saturday cartoons and the classic AM radio stations that played classic Rock & Roll music. There is always a reference to the Motown Sound and the Super Soul music of the 1970's.

He was the camp coordinator always putting together fun activities for family and friends, a college radio Disc Jockey and concert promoter and friend to Black or White, demanding to be treated right. John Gary, as the North and South Carolina family called him, is an inclusive leader who is not afraid to praise the Lord and is in-the-book.

John Gary Dewberry Jr, it rhymes, it's in sync and it sits in Block, ready for print, and he is excited for you to enjoy this first of its kind story. Welcome to Soul Sonnets.